TRUMP'S ENEMIES

How the Deep State Is Undermining the Presidency

COREY R. LEWANDOWSKI
AND DAVID N. BOSSIE

CENTER
STREET

NEW YORK NASHVILLE

Center Street
Hachette Book Group
1290 Avenue of the Americas, New York, NY 10104
centerstreet.com
twitter.com/centerstreet

First published in hardcover and ebook in November 2018.
First Trade Paperback Edition: December 2019

Center Street is a division of Hachette Book Group, Inc. The Center Street name and logo are trademarks of Hachette Book Group, Inc.

The publisher is not responsible for websites (or their content) that are not owned by the publisher.

The Hachette Speakers Bureau provides a wide range of authors for speaking events. To find out more, go to www.HachetteSpeakersBureau.com or call (866) 376-6591.

Print book interior design by Timothy Shaner, NightandDayDesign.biz

Library of Congress Cataloging-in-Publication Data has been applied for.

ISBNs: 978-1-5460-7620-9 (trade paperback), 978-1-5460-7621-6 (ebook)

Printed in the United States of America

LSC-C

10 9 8 7 6 5 4 3 2 1

TO THE HARDWORKING MEN AND WOMEN
OF THE UNITED STATES:

WE CONTINUE TO FIGHT THE DEEP STATE,
THE SWAMP CREATURES, THE FAKE NEWS
AND CORRUPT UNELECTED BUREAUCRATS
WHO ATTEMPT TO SUBVERT THE WILL OF
THE PEOPLE—WE WILL DRAIN THE SWAMP!!!

COREY R. LEWANDOWSKI
To my family, especially my wife and children who
supported me during the Witch Hunt: You have my
gratitude and love more than you will ever know.
To my mother who always taught me to fight for
what I believe in.

To my brother Carl, for your decades of
service to our country in the USMC.
Thank you!

DAVID N. BOSSIE
To my family: my incredible wife, Susan,
and our wonderful children, Isabella, Griffin,
Lily, and Maggie. I love you all!

And to my parents, who taught me
to put America First.

CONTENTS

INTRODUCTION TO THE TRADE EDITION

If you haven't read the Mueller report yet, don't bother. We know that it's been in the news lately, and that those heavy paperback copies are probably pretty cheap right about now. In fact, if you're flipping through this introduction in a bookstore, you're probably only a few steps away from a big stack of discounted Mueller reports, likely printed by the *Washington Post* or some other Fake News organization looking to spread false allegations about the president. (Don't be fooled by how many copies are still sitting around, by the way; that's just what happens to unwanted books before they get fed into the big wood-chipper in the store parking lot.)

As a kind of public service, we've gone through the Mueller report page by mind-numbing page, looking for any sign of wrongdoing by anyone, just so innocent readers like you won't have to. Aside from a few mentions of Corey's name, we found nothing even remotely interesting.

Take it from us: This thing is not worth your time.

Seriously. Even if you leave everything else aside—the FISA abuse, the fake dossier, the attempted coup—the report is just plain boring. You'd have more fun watching Sleepy Joe Biden read out of the phonebook. If you're at all interested, we recommend just waiting for the movie. (We hear Mark Wahlberg is in early talks to play Corey, but let's keep that between us.) Until then, we suggest that you kick back with this book, *Trump's Enemies*, and learn the real story.

This book goes behind the headlines and between the lines of the Mueller report. It reveals the truth behind the fake Russia collusion investigation—how it came about, why it failed, and why no one who was involved with this massive conspiracy should get away with it. It covers everything from the former spies who started the Russia rumors, the corrupt journalists who helped spread them, and the swamp creatures from all over Washington who tried and failed to remove Donald J. Trump from office.

Trump's Enemies is the real story—and while it may be a bit complex, it's the most important story of our lives. (Even if you don't think so, at least this one is short.) By the time it's over, you'll be as convinced as we are that serious action needs to be taken. It's time to investigate the investigators.

When we started writing this book, the rumors about the Deep State and its war on President Trump were really just that—rumors. They were things that people said to each other only in private, speaking softly over the dinner tables and desks in our nation's capital. No one could prove any of it was true. No one could say for sure, for instance, that there really *was* a small group of corrupt establishment and FBI officials trying to stop President Trump from succeeding, stalling every one of his policies through legislative slow-rolling and outright insubordination. Certainly, no one could know that the intelligence community under Barack Obama had completely fabricated the Russia collusion story in order to cover up for Hillary Clinton's loss and deem Donald J. Trump an illegitimate president. Anyone who tried was either stonewalled by the system or just laughed out of the room.

But we did the work. We spoke with officials from the highest ranks of the government and the private sector to find out the truth. Many of these people spoke under conditions of anonymity, and at great risk to their reputations. But eventually, they gave us the pieces of the puzzle, and we put it together in the pages of this book.

What follows is a step-by-step account of how rogue agents at the FBI, the CIA, and the Obama White House joined forces to attempt a coup on the presidency of the United States. It's the story of how Hillary Clinton's campaign paid an opposition research group called Fusion GPS to dig up dirt on Donald J. Trump when he was still a candidate, and how that single act brought about the entire Russia collusion delusion. From there, the story goes all over the globe, from a small seminar room on the campus of Cambridge University to the hallowed halls of the White House and back again. It covers the miscarriages of justice that occurred under James Comey, the disgraced former director of the FBI who will soon (we hope) be brought up on criminal charges for his conduct. It covers the escapades of FBI lovers Peter Strzok and Lisa Page, two key figures in the Mueller investigation who have a long and well-documented desire to take down President Trump.

It also goes deep into the history of Robert Mueller, a man we now know had very little to do with the report that bears his name—and his incestuous relationship with Comey, Clapper, and other members of the Deep State. After watching the dumpster fire of a Senate hearing, during which he was forced yet again by Democrats to speak about the results of his report, it is clear that he was the author of the Mueller report in name only, and that he was little more than a figurehead for the whole crooked operation. For what it's worth, it also doesn't seem like he was exactly "all there." It was actually sad. Watching that hearing was like watching someone yell at a confused old man in a language he doesn't know.

But beyond the Russia investigation—beyond the obviously illegal actions of the Democrats and a stunning dereliction of duty by the mainstream media—this is a book about a president who has managed to succeed in the face of stunning obstacles. All along, while the Democrats were running with the collusion story every day, hoping the president would simply give in to the pressure and resign, President Trump remained strong, repeating the same four words over and over again: *No collusion. No obstruction.* Even when the 2018 midterm elections came along and his party took a massive hit at the ballot box—largely thanks to the specter of the Russia collusion hoax—he didn't change his tune. He just kept working on behalf of the American people. Now that we're on the other side of the Mueller report and the truth is out in the open, he's been proven completely correct at every turn, and the levels of enthusiasm for him from the American people have never been higher.

CAST OF CHARACTERS

STEPHEN K. BANNON: Former Chief Strategist to President Donald J. Trump

CORY BOOKER: U.S. Senator from New Jersey

DAVID N. BOSSIE: Former Deputy Campaign Manager to Donald J. Trump for President

JOHN BRENNAN: Former Director of the Central Intelligence Agency (CIA)

JAMES CLAPPER: Former Director of the National Intelligence (DNI)

HILLARY R. CLINTON: Former Secretary of State of the United States and former First Lady

GARY COHN: Former President of Goldman Sachs and Director of the NEC under President Trump

JAMES COMEY: Former Director of the FBI

JOHNNY DESTEFANO: Assistant to the President and Counselor to President Donald J. Trump

JEFF FLAKE: U.S. Senator from Arizona

MICHAEL J. FLYNN: Former National Security Advisor to President Donald J. Trump

HOPE HICKS: Former Director of Strategic Communications under President Trump

STEFAN HALPER: College Professor who recruited spies for CIA and MI6

KAMALA HARRIS: U.S. Senator from California

GENERAL JOHN KELLY: Assistant to the President and Chief of Staff to President Donald J. Trump

COREY R. LEWANDOWSKI: Former Campaign Manager to Donald J. Trump for President

ANDREW MCCABE: Former Deputy Director of the FBI

JEFF MERKLEY: U.S. Senator from Oregon

STEPHEN MILLER: Assistant to the President and Senior Advisor to President Donald J. Trump

ROBERT MUELLER: Former Director of the FBI and Special Counsel of Russia Investigation

BARACK OBAMA: 44th President of the United States

BRUCE OHR: Former Associate Deputy Attorney General and Director of Organized Crime Drug Enforcement Task Force (OCDETF) under President Obama. Husband of Nellie Ohr

NELLIE OHR: Wife of Bruce Ohr and employee of Fusion GPS

CARTER PAGE: Trump campaign volunteer whom the DOJ spied on

LISA PAGE: Former FBI Attorney and mistress of Peter Strzok

GEORGE PAPADOPOULOS: Trump campaign volunteer

NANCY PELOSI: Minority Leader of the House of Representatives

ROB PORTER: Former Staff Secretary to President Donald J. Trump

REINCE PRIEBUS: Former Chief of Staff to President Donald J. Trump

ROD ROSENSTEIN: Deputy Attorney General of the United States

SUSAN RICE: Former National Security Advisor under President Barack Obama

SARAH HUCKABEE SANDERS: Assistant to the President and Press Secretary to President Donald J. Trump

BEN SASSE: U.S. Senator from Nebraska

DAN SCAVINO: Assistant to the President and Director of Social Media to President Donald J. Trump

ADAM SCHIFF: U.S. Representative from California

JEFF SESSIONS: Attorney General of the United States

GLENN SIMPSON: Former American Journalist and
  founder of Fusion GPS

BILL STEPIAN: Deputy Assistant to the President and
  White House Political Director

PETER STRZOK: Former Chief of the Counterespionage
  section of the FBI and paramour of Lisa Page

ERIC SWALWELL: U.S. Representative from California

DONALD J. TRUMP: 45th President of the United States

MELANIA TRUMP: First Lady of the United States

ELIZABETH WARREN: U.S. Senator from
  Massachusetts

MAXINE WATERS: U.S. Representative from California

SALLY YATES: Former Deputy Attorney General under
  President Barack Obama

CHAPTER 1

THE PRESIDENT

THURSDAY, SEPTEMBER 20, 2018. We arrived at the 17th and State Street appointments entrance of the White House complex around 3:30 p.m. Our interview with the president was set for 3:45, so we only had a few minutes to get through security and into the Oval Office. We had spent all day preparing for it, drafting questions and wondering how to best use the forty-five minutes the White House had scheduled for us with the boss. We've both had conversations with the president countless times, but this one would be different.

The idea for the interview began a couple of months before while we were riding with the president in Beast, the name given to the presidential limousine. That day we had accompanied President Trump to a rally in Evansville, Indiana, and were headed back to Air Force One. In the Beast we mentioned to the president that Major Garrett of CBS News had a book coming out in the near future.

Despite what the Fake News will tell you, Donald J. Trump is unbelievably accessible to the media. During the campaign he did over seven hundred interviews with the *New York Times* alone. The president told us he wanted to talk with Major about his book. Major's book, however, was due out in a couple of weeks—it was far too late for the president to be interviewed. We also knew that Major had tried to get a sit-down with the president but people in the White House had stonewalled him. It was another example of staff making decisions that were detrimental to the president.

The president shook his head.

"Why the hell does this keep happening?" he asked.

He had already gone through an identical situation a few days before, with Bob Woodward and his book. That book, too, had already been written by the time the president found out that Woodward wanted to speak with him.

"Bob Woodward wants to talk to me and he's getting told no," the president said. "What am I, too much of a big shot to talk to Woodward? I can't return that guy's call?" The president was clearly irritated that he wasn't getting his messages.

The president had believed, and rightly so, that without his input Woodward's book would portray him and the White House in a negative light. The book is filled with inaccuracies and lies from disgruntled former staffers.

We mentioned to the president we were writing a new book and told him the title and described what we were working on. He immediately instructed us to come in to see him to discuss it in greater detail.

Following this conversation, we contacted Bill Shine, the Deputy White House Chief of Staff for Communications, to set up a formal interview with the president. Shine confirmed our conversation with the boss and organized the interview.

We set out to tell the true story of the Trump White House from the point of view of two people who know the president well. In *Let Trump Be Trump*, we hadn't asked the president to participate in an interview because we respect the important work he is doing and didn't want to take away from that. Once he got word of what was in Woodward's book, however, and all the lies and misstatements about the White House contained therein, we asked him if he wanted to sit down for an interview about his enemies to set the record straight.

At the White House there was an extensive line to pass through the Secret Service security checkpoint, longer than anything either of us had seen before. It was easily a forty-five-minute wait. The problem was we only had fifteen minutes before the interview itself. Luckily for us, one of the people at the front of the line invited us to join him. We learned from him that the reason for the long line was the White House was hosting a conference for student veterans.

Once we passed through the initial checkpoint, we met our escort, Meghan McCann. Because there are still people who work at the White House who are intimidated by our relationship with the president, we must have an escort whenever we are on the complex. Today was no different. Even though we had an appointment with the president himself we were still required to have an escort. Meghan had heard us complain about this ridiculous insult to us— that no one else that we know of has to have. It's now a running joke among the members of the Secret Service who work at the West Wing checkpoint.

Meghan escorted us to the upstairs West Wing lobby where Bill Shine and Sarah Huckabee Sanders came out to greet us. On our way in to the Oval Office, we said hello to Hogan Gidley and Laura Nasim of the communications team and our old friend Dan Scavino.

Inside the Oval Office, there were four chairs facing the Resolute Desk. As we walked in, the boss greeted us warmly, as old friends. We took the middle two; Bill Shine sat to Dave's left while Sarah Huckabee Sanders sat to Corey's right. We knew that in about forty-five minutes, the president would be boarding Marine One on the south lawn for the eleven-minute flight to Joint Base Andrews. We witnessed the staggering amount of Fake News the president has to contend with: Bob Woodward's book had hit the shelves. Additionally, a gutless op-ed written under the byline "Anonymous" had been published in the *New York Times*. It was a perfect day to talk about Trump's enemies.

America was working again, and we were safer than ever. Dave mentioned the stock market was about to hit an all-time high and break another new record, one that no one had ever thought possible. Corey turned to the list of questions we'd prepared and Dave placed his phone on the Resolute Desk to record the conversation but, before we could start, the president wanted to talk about the market, which he had been watching rise to new heights since the day he was elected. "It'll close at the all-time record again," he said. "We had the all-time record, then it went down a little when I did the trade stuff. Now it's right back up. Shows you how bad tariffs are, right?"

For months, the mainstream media had been criticizing the president's fair trade policies, saying the stock market would plummet if they were ever implemented—exactly what they used to say would happen if he got elected in the first place. Everyone in the room laughed, as the market had climbed to its highest point in history. Corey turned back to his questions, asking the boss about the first years of his presidency, the Fake News, and all the enemies that have lined up against him since he was elected. His answers were revealing, and all given in the same candid, plainspoken style that propelled him to victory.

During the interview, Dave asked the president about his new legal team—the ones who were fighting for him every night on television against the onslaught of the Mueller probe and the media. He seemed happy to be taking a more combative stance to the fake Russia investigation.

"You guys know better than anybody," the president said. "There was no collusion. You know that Bob Woodward's book started about collusion? But he had one problem. Do you know what his problem was?"

Corey, who'd heard about Woodward's failure to uncover anything on the Russian collusion story, was the first to answer the president.

"It didn't exist," he said. "The same thing happened to him that happens to everybody else."

The president nodded, obviously amused by the whole Russia hoax that was going on around him. "Look," he said. "I don't think he's a very good reporter, personally. But I blame myself because I didn't talk to him. Nobody told me that he was trying to talk to me. Because I have a lot of people who want to talk to me."

For the next forty-five minutes, we asked the president questions about everything from his regrets and accomplishments to the dishonest way he's often portrayed in the media. He answered honestly, and didn't try to sugarcoat any of his responses. This is the only formal book interview President Trump has sat for since being elected to office, and we were honored to be the ones who conducted it. We left the building with the recorded interview on our phones. We could hardly believe how lucky the two of us were to have just interviewed the leader of the free world in the Oval Office.

There is perhaps no one in the president's political orbit who knows him better than we do. During the 2016 Donald J. Trump for President campaign, we (Dave, as deputy campaign manager, and Corey, as campaign manager for the first eighteen months of the campaign) flew hundreds of thousands of miles with then-candidate Trump. Dave will tell you, as Election Day drew near, "Trump Force One," Mr. Trump's personal souped-up 757 jet, zigzagged across the country like a pinball, making four, five or even six stops a day. As we described in our first book, *Let Trump Be Trump*, life on Trump Force One was, well, unique. On any given flight, you might be sitting across from Don King, Bobby Knight, or Lou Holtz while Elton John's "Tiny Dancer" played at ear-splitting levels on the sound system. We subsisted on Vienna Fingers and diet Coke. We were an army of misfit toys, outgunned, outmanned, and outspent at every turn. At 30,000 feet, however, we blew them all away.

A lot has happened since the campaign. During his first year and a half in office, the president has nominated two Supreme Court justices, and sent the economy skyrocketing. He also brought a big, polished set of balls back to American foreign policy, meeting face-to-face with Kim Jong Un of North Korea to bring the world closer to peace.

A historic tax cut bill, unprecedented federal regulatory reform, and fair trade policy, it's been amazing to watch!

He managed to accomplish all of this in the face of a Washington swamp that hums with self-interested bureaucrats, political operators, and cynical politicians, many of whom are working every day to stop the America First agenda. Unelected bureaucrats, in agencies like the EPA and the Department of Agriculture, are trying to stall the president's priorities at every turn, even refusing direct orders. Some of the people in the White House, it was now becoming clear, couldn't, and shouldn't, be trusted. Then there was the constant assault by Fake News, the liberal elites, and the Democrats, all of whom have a stake in seeing President Trump and by extension our country fail.

Most egregious of all of Trump's enemies, however, are the rogue members of the intelligence complex (IC). Led by former CIA Director John Brennan, the upper echelons of the IC and federal law enforcement have waged a full-on war against the president. The fiction of Russian collusion has been the culmination of their efforts.

What follows in the pages ahead is our first-person account of the war against President Donald J. Trump, which is being waged at various levels of the intelligence community, the halls of the Congress, and even from inside the White House itself.

For the purposes of making this story as easy as possible to follow, we have ironed out a lot of what we're about to tell, arranging the facts chronologically so they would be easier to understand. In reality, much of what follows came to us in small drips and whispers from around the capital and a few rare conservative enclaves in the media. We had to rely on several sources from inside the government and the intelligence community, who came to us on deep background, and much of what we found out was actively suppressed by Democrats in Congress. Someday, we could write a whole book on the sordid details of uncovering these facts; but for now, you should find the information itself shocking enough.

We did.

Ahead is a story about the profound arrogance of power-hungry reptiles who think that they're more important than the votes of more than 60 million people. It is a story about a stain that spreads from the highest reaches of law enforcement to lowly bureaucrats with the access they should have never been given in the first place. It is the story of a biased media that seeks not the truth but ratings and readers. It's a story we again tell in one voice.

And it's a story that begins four years ago in a famous university north of London . . .

CHAPTER 2

DINNER AT CAMBRIDGE

ON A COLD NIGHT in February 2014 at Cambridge University—the same place where Christopher Steele had been trained in dossier writing and espionage—about a dozen spies and foreign policy scholars held a dinner in Michael Flynn's honor. It was held in a long seminar hall. Flynn had just finished a tour of Europe on behalf of the Obama administration, and wanted to make one last stop to catch up with his European counterparts.

When Flynn arrived, Sir Richard Dearlove, the former head of the secret British intelligence service known as MI6, brought him around the room and made introductions. The people in the banquet hall were virtually strangers to Flynn. They knew him, however, mostly by reputation. Flynn was then the director of the Defense Intelligence Agency (DIA), the branch of the United States military that gathers intelligence on terrorist groups and hostile actors in foreign countries. Under Flynn, the DIA had begun honing its focus on radical Islamic terrorism, working with agents in Russia to fight ISIS in Iraq and Syria. In some circles, he was a rock star.

The old-school spies, however, were leery of him.

Most of the attendees were actually spies-turned-academics who had come to Cambridge University around 2004 and named themselves the "Cambridge Security Initiative." Many of them had lived through the proxy wars of the 1950s and '60s, then the Cuban Missile Crisis, as well as several poisonings of Russian nationals on British soil. All this left a bad taste in their mouths—an idea of Russia as the eternal aggressor, a meddler in foreign affairs. Putin had just annexed Ukraine a few days earlier, and word around the room was that he had his sights on the Crimean Peninsula next. Putin was not one of their favorite individuals.

One of the old snoops in the room was a foreign policy scholar and senior fellow at Cambridge named Stefan Halper, a disheveled, portly man who had an obsession with American spy culture. He had spent some time in the 1980s running intelligence operations for Presidents Reagan and Carter, and he'd married the daughter of a famous CIA agent. That night, he was one of the few people in history to have attained two full professorships: one at a branch of Cambridge called Magdalen College, and another at Stanford University in California. In both places, he kept an eye out for young talent, scouting new spies for American and British intelligence services.

Halper and his friends at MI6 were skeptical of Flynn. They had watched tensions among the United States, Iran, and Russia reach a boiling point during the sloppy, under-the-table negotiations that took place for Obama's Iran nuclear deal, and they were worried about escalation. The dinner at Cambridge had been organized, in large part, so that British agents could get a feel for who Flynn was, how he might be useful to them later. They wanted to remind him who his friends were. It was difficult for them to envision a world in which an agent of United States intelligence could trust a Russian more than, say, someone who wore moth-eaten suits and smoked a pipe in the gray-brick towers of Cambridge University. They believed data was collected in well-lit rooms like the one they were in that night, communicated via cables and coded messages rather than done on the ground by way of networking and making connections.

They were the establishment, just like their Deep State friends in the American Federal Bureau of Investigation (FBI), Central Intelligence Agency (CIA), and National Security Agency (NSA). The problem with being the establishment, with holding on to your place within the organization you're part of, is that you become stagnant. You learn all you know in the first ten years of your career and then spend the next forty repeating the same lines you've memorized. If Russia is the ultimate enemy when you take your first job in 1975, you'll keep thinking that until you retire in 2025. Flynn was the exact opposite. He changed as the situation dictated, often taking meetings no other intelligence officer who had political aims would take. He had more conversations per minute than any other DIA chief in history, and he was about to have one more—one that would change the course of his career forever.

When the chatter settled down, and dinner began, Flynn found himself seated a few places down from a young woman with blond hair, no more than thirty-five years old. She had a few file folders on the table in front of her, one of which had handwritten notes inside.

He soon learned that her name was Svetlana Lokhova and that she was a graduate student at Cambridge in history. She spoke with a thick Russian accent. A few minutes into the meal, Halper asked her to talk about the project she was working on.

She told the room that she was writing a book, something that would use archival material from Moscow and tell the story of various spy programs from the 1920s and '30s. The information she needed in Russia was carefully guarded, especially since Vladimir Putin took office, but she said she had been allowed exclusive access into the archives of the Kremlin and other government agencies.

The book, she said, would tell the Soviet side of the famous Cambridge Spy Ring story. The story involved a professor at Cambridge University who recruited several undergraduates into the communist security service, who, after World War II broke out, were able to infiltrate British intelligence agencies.

After her presentation, Svetlana and Flynn began to talk. You can't blame the general for chatting with her, a beautiful, fascinating woman in a room filled with stodgy old men. Before the night was over, Flynn gave her his email addresses. Over the next few months, Flynn and Svetlana exchanged a few emails. In a couple of them, Flynn signed off as "General Misha," using the Russian word for Michael as a joke. She would update him on the progress of the book. That was about the sum and substance of their relationship.

The spies, however, were watching. And they didn't like what they saw. By the time Flynn boarded his plane back to the United States, there were spies digging into this Russian graduate student's past. Clearly, they suspected her of being a spy, although none of them said anything.

And they wouldn't—not in so many words, and not for about two years.

CHAPTER 3

THE HANDOFF

IN THE AFTERMATH of the election, while we were dealing with our staffing dilemmas over at Trump Tower, the Clinton team was busy clearing out its campaign headquarters in downtown Brooklyn. They removed hundreds of thousands of dollars' worth of opposition research and polling data and shredded it, then cleared out the offices of a few hundred well-paid staffers and closed the doors for good. We can only imagine how much that must have stung. They had just blown, as the media and the rest of the experts told them, what should have been a slam dunk for their party, and the whole world had watched them do it. Had it been the other way around, and we were the ones clearing out our headquarters in shame, we might have skulked away and stayed quiet for a while.

But the Clinton campaign, in characteristic fashion, did exactly the opposite. It wasn't long before their spokespeople were back in conference rooms trying to think of excuses for the loss, which didn't take very long at all. They said that the Trump campaign must have cheated, that former FBI director James Comey's October email surprise was a fatal blow, and that the media had given our campaign more coverage than it should have. But those reasons were all small potatoes compared to the big enchilada, which they dropped on the Friday after the election and haven't stopped talking about since.

We're talking about the fake Russian collusion, of course, a sweeping work of fiction so complex, so audacious, so unbelievable, that if they gave out awards for bad excuses, the Democrats would win an Oscar, an Emmy, and maybe even the Heisman Trophy.

You've probably heard all about it, but in case you were living on Mars, here are the salient points: Vladimir Putin, who hates Hillary Clinton as much as anyone on earth, ordered a bunch of secret agents in Russia to hire a few thousand computer nerds and midlevel hackers. Those hackers were trained by the Russian government to create funny anti-Clinton picture "memes" on Facebook—and post them all over American political groups on the internet. Then . . . well, actually, that's it. Just a few thousand Facebook ads and some computer "hackers." This, ladies and gentlemen, is the sum and substance of this attack that Democrats have compared to Pearl Harbor and 9/11.

You have to admit, though, for a story they came up with in a couple of days, it was pretty ingenious. With longtime operatives like Sidney Blumenthal, who tried to smear Monica Lewinsky for the Clintons, and Cody Shearer, the son of a gossip columnist who calls himself a journalist but is as much of a reporter as Michael Wolff, and plenty of friends in Obama's administration, Hillary's people had to know about Paul Manafort's and Rick Gates' sketchy ties to Russian oligarchs. They must have thought that it was enough to get the story rolling. But still, as stories go, it was all very sloppy in the beginning. It was as if the Clinton campaign had hired a second-rate spy novelist to do post-election public relations, then published the craziest parts of their first draft without reading them. We never thought anyone could really buy it.

But the press ate it up. By Christmas, Russian collusion was liberal gospel. Believers were quoted in the *New York Times,* and nonbelievers became anti-American, Russian sympathizers, or worse. Newspapers on news-stands all around Trump Tower had photos of Putin and laptop computers on their covers. Fifth Avenue was lined with declarations of a new cold war.

Barack Obama sent his press secretary, Josh Earnest, out to the podium in the White House briefing room, to help stoke the fire. Earnest accused Trump of not only knowing about the Russians hacking the election, but of helping them. "First of all, it is just a fact—you have it all on tape—that the Republican nominee for president was encouraging Russia to hack his opponent because he believed that that would help his campaign," he said.

Then, nine days after the election, Obama stood next to German chancellor Angela Merkel and threw lighter fluid on the fire: "Mr. Trump obviously knew that Russia was engaged in malicious cyber activity that was helping him and hurting Secretary Clinton's campaign," he said.

This was nuts. How could all these people believe this junk? To us, it always came down to a single question, which no one on the left could ever answer. How many votes did the Russians change on election day? The comparatively tiny amount of ads they took out on Facebook were ridiculous. In one, Jesus is shown punching Hillary Clinton. Come on. Mr. Trump won the Electoral College by seventy-four votes—a blowout!

But the Democrats, the establishment, and the media needed a story, and the Clintons, with the help of the Obama administration, got to work making the one about Russia seem plausible. They built up the Russian collusion narrative the way a Russian mail-order bride builds up her online dating profile. The "case" had intrigue, espionage, and the best clickbait known to man—weird sex. So it was outlandish, they thought. So what? By the time anyone got to the truth, the damage would already have been done and maybe, just maybe they would be able to reverse the outcome of the election. Crazy, right? They didn't think it was, believe us.

Still, for the first few weeks after the election, the Russia story was barely a blip on the radar. From what we heard, some people had met with diplomats and forgotten to record or disclose the conversations. Paul Manafort, being the swamp creature that he is, was revealed to have had illegal ties from many years ago with Ukrainian businessmen. None of it had anything to do with Donald Trump.

All we knew was that no one had colluded, cooperated, or coordinated—whatever that meant—with a foreign power. In the early days of the campaign, Corey could barely get his socks to match, he was so busy. By the time Dave came aboard in August 2016, the campaign was so demanding we had enough trouble keeping the schedule straight. There was no coordination with a hostile power planning a takeover of the White House.

By the end of 2016, we all figured the Russia story would blow over. We thought the Obama administration would give us a full report, enumerate the supposed "damages," and leave it to the new president to decide what to do about Russia and Putin. Given the fact that Barack Obama was a lame-duck president, this would have been more in line with historical precedent. That isn't what happened, however. Instead, the Obama administration decided on taking drastic action, the motivation for which is still in question. What isn't in question are the repercussions of Obama's actions, which we're still dealing with today.

December 29, 2016. Dave had taken a couple of days over Christmas to take his family to Alabama. He has a hunting cabin in Marengo County, where his wife, Susan, grew up. It was the first time he'd taken his foot off the pedal since he joined the Donald J. Trump for President campaign the previous August. Although it was only a little more than four months, the time he spent helping Trump get elected president felt both like a lifetime and the blink of an eye. He more than deserved the time off. Though he didn't expect the short holiday to be one of total peace and quiet, he figured he could limit the calamities coming out of the transition to just one a day. As it turned out, he was right. He could almost tell by the urgent way his BlackBerry was buzzing that it was Stephen K. Bannon calling. Bannon was at Mar-a-Lago, a Trump residence in Palm Peach, Florida, with the president-elect.

"It's going to lead to a constitutional crisis," he said, almost breathlessly.

If you knew Bannon as long as we have, you would know that just about everything is "going to lead to a constitutional crisis." He's not always right, but he's right enough times to make you sit up and listen.

Bannon said the Obama administration was about to expel thirty-five Russian diplomats from the country as retaliation for the supposed cyberattacks carried out by Russia. It was going to happen before the end of the day. There had been no word of this from the White House, and Bannon said it hadn't been in the Presidential Daily Briefing (PDB) for that day.

The PDB was a digital compilation of top-secret analysis and suggested actions from the intelligence complex that both President Obama and, now, President-elect Trump, looked at several times a week. It came on an iPad. Other than a tiny team at the Pentagon, who decided very early in the morning what went in and what didn't go in, almost no one had access to the PDB. Why those few, acting on their own with political motivations, or on orders from higher-ups, kept that little tidbit from us we don't know. What seemed apparent, however, was that somebody didn't want those of us on the transition team to know about what was going to happen that day, so they conveniently left out the expulsion of the Russians.

Bannon found out by reading the newspaper, just like everyone else.

"This is insane," he said. "We didn't even do this at the height of the Cold War. In 1983, we were seconds away from launching missiles at each other, and we didn't do this. How is Russia a bigger enemy now than they were then?"

Before Dave could answer, Bannon was yelling to Reince Priebus, who was in Mar-a-Lago with him.

"I want a meeting," Bannon said. "I want a meeting with every intelligence officer and anyone who touched this Russia shit. We're going to get to the bottom of this."

Bannon called Denis McDonough, the chief of staff at the Obama White House. McDonough picked up on the second ring, almost as if he'd been expecting the call. What he couldn't have expected was the beating he was about to take. Steve told him what he'd told Dave, barely stopping for breath, then made some demands.

"Here's what I want," he said. "I'm going to fly down there this afternoon, and you're going to show me exactly the presentation that President Obama got. And I want to talk to every person who briefed him on this."

For about ten years in the 1980s, Steve Bannon was an aide to the chief of naval operations (CNO) at the Pentagon. In other words, he was well versed in every aspect of the military intel and statecraft. He knew if the president of the United States made a decision of the magnitude that Obama just had, there had to have been a presentation of some kind—something that would have been official, stamped by every intelligence agency involved, then entered into the historical record when the decision was rendered. That was—and still is—the law.

And that's what Bannon wanted to see.

McDonough didn't know what he was up against. He started with something Steve calls the humanahumanahumana routine, the one that Jackie Gleason made famous in his 1950's sitcom, *The Honeymooners*. When McDonough finally found his footing, he said something about it being complicated, and that the presentation was coming, but that lots of people are involved in these decisions, et cetera, et cetera. Bannon had heard enough.

"Stop," he said. "I just want to see the presentation. If Obama saw ten pages, I want to see the ten pages; if he got a hundred, I want to see a hundred. No more, no less. If there was a PowerPoint, show me that."

After a few more minutes of mumbling and obfuscation from the White House—most of it spent on hold— something became clear to Steve.

There had never been a presentation to Obama.

The folks in the Obama White House had about as much concrete knowledge of Russian hacking as we have of French poetry. The whole decision to kick out Russian diplomats must have been little more than a ploy to keep their false Russia narrative afloat, something that'd make their decision to keep the investigation just a little more plausible and unimpeachable. This way, when the Obama holdovers in the Department of Justice called for a lengthy and expensive investigation by a special prosecutor, everyone would believe it was vital. No one would bat an eye. After such drastic action, toward an enemy that "attacked" our democracy, it would be downright treasonous to question its legitimacy. Boy oh boy, these guys were good.

Needless to say, Steve Bannon didn't fly to D.C. that day. There would have been nothing for him to see. In looking back, it's clear that we probably should have caused more of a stink. We had a few other things on our mind, however, like conducting the business of building a government. Inauguration day was fast approaching, and we only had about four thousand government appointments to fill.

Still, with each day that passed, like dark, heavy clouds building before the storm, the specter of a potential Russia investigation increased. Everyone knew we hadn't seen the last of the phony collusion story. If they wanted to, the Obama holdovers in their various administrative roles could keep it going until they started a full-on war. The question was whether the people we hired to work in our White House and the various national security organizations of the executive branch could do anything to stop them.

As it turned out, not everyone in those places wanted to stop them.

The White House called back a few days later. It seemed they had finally gotten their story straight, and they wanted to set up a meeting on Russian hacking.

McDonough suggested President Trump have a briefing with every intel agency who'd had even a glancing acquaintance with the Russia stuff. This meant that the heads of the top three intelligence and federal law enforcement organizations—John Brennan of the Central Intelligence Agency (CIA), James Clapper, director of national intelligence (DNI), and James Comey of the Federal Bureau of Investigation (FBI)—would come together and brief the president-elect on their findings. This way, he said, there'd be nothing unspoken between the incoming administration and the outgoing one. They'd be working from the same material, looking at the same notes.

At first, Bannon refused.

"I don't want that," he said. "Obama didn't get that. Give me exactly what he got."

When Bannon got his teeth into something, he was like a dog with a bone.

Though they still wouldn't admit that Obama never got the briefing, the meeting was their idea of a consolation prize. The heads of all three federal agencies would come and brief Donald Trump on everything they knew about Russian hacking and lay out their reasons for expelling the diplomats.

Of course, they didn't tell Mr. Trump about the surprise that James Comey had in store for him.

January 6, 2017, was a chilly, overcast day that felt like snow in New York City. Since the election, the street-level floor of the atrium of Trump Tower was filled with significant Secret Service presence, the press, and tourists who were treated to a daily stream of famous faces from business and politics. On this day, the media was staked out to see America's intelligence chiefs but missed them because they entered Trump Tower from the residence side. Once in the building, they took the elevators up to the twenty-fourth floor, got off, and headed to a separate elevator bank that took them up to the twenty-fifth floor.

The director of national intelligence came out of the elevator first. Clapper walked slowly and purposefully, eyes nearly shut, his top lip sinking into the bottom one like he was trying to eat it. He looked like a fish that had been on the deck of a boat for a while. Behind him came John O. Brennan, the red-faced director of the CIA. There seemed to be about four hundred collective years between them. Together they gave the impression of a couple of guys who have been doing what they're doing for too long. They walked into the conference room in tandem. Mr. Trump was waiting for them.

But it was neither Clapper nor Brennan who changed the course of history. That person was the man in the dark suit who ducked out of the elevator behind his two compatriots, the man who in one short meeting would set in motion a conspiracy that would seek to cause critical damage to the presidency, the man who would go on to lie to the American people, the man with whom Dave once worked investigating Hillary Clinton—that man was James Comey.

When Dave worked as a congressional investigator, he lived in Firehouse Station 15 in Burtonsville, Maryland, where he slept on a bottom bunk. No joke. He did. From 1990 to 2000 he answered several thousands of emergency calls while living in the firehouse. It was a simpler time. There were no cell phones then—at least Dave didn't have one—so he would do the business of a congressional investigator over the firehouse phone. When he was out on a call, the guys at the firehouse would write messages for him on scraps of paper or write them on a whiteboard. On one memorable occasion, he walked in to find that someone had left him a note on the whiteboard that read "Nute" had called.

"Nute?"

It took Dave a couple of seconds before he realized they meant "Newt" as in Gingrich, the Speaker of the House.

When Newt Gingrich called it was usually a pretty serious matter. On that particular occasion, around 1996, he was checking on Dave's progress regarding an investigation into the Clintons, something he had been working on for a few months. He and his team were getting a whole lot of heat from the White House, and Newt was starting to become annoyed.

To refresh your memory, when Bill Clinton was elected president of the United States in 1992, rumors of extramarital affairs and corruption—in his home state of Arkansas—were rampant. Dozens of women had already accused him of extramarital affairs, most of whom lived in the state where he was the most powerful man. Other people reported shady business dealings with him. Even Hillary, who had barely been in the public eye long enough back then to have any name recognition, had gotten into some trouble. In 1978, she had invested $1,000 with a friend named Red Bone in cattle futures, wanting to make a little extra cash. The word "extra" doesn't quite capture what transpired. Less than a year later, the investment of a grand had ballooned, somehow, to $100,000. The chances of a payoff like that, even under the most favorable conditions, were about one in 31 trillion—really, Dave had a mathematician tell him that. Everyone knew the Clintons were dirty, but no one could make anything stick. They were really good at getting away with stuff and people had no idea how.

Then, in 1994, Senate investigators found something that looked promising while investigating the Clintons' "Whitewater" land deal. On top of that, Vince Foster had died of an apparent suicide. Foster had been a friend of the Clintons for many years and Deputy White House counsel for the first six months of the administration. The Clintons, together with two friends, James and Susan McDougal, invested in a property at the confluence of the White River and, appropriately, Crooked Creek. James, known as Jim to his friends, took out two large loans to pay for it. When the project failed due to the economy and a lousy location, Jim defrauded a small savings-and-loan association he bought as a front to the tune of about $3 million. When the bank failed, it cost the taxpayers about $73 million. The McDougals were convicted, and evidence showed the

Clintons had been involved, which set off an independent counsel investigation.

Concurrent with the independent counsel's investigation, which was by then run by Kenneth Starr, the U.S. Senate began its own investigation of the Whitewater land deal—one that had a broad scope and was in the public eye. Alfonse D'Amato, "Pothole Al," a famously outspoken Republican senator from Long Island, served as chairman of the committee. He hired Mike Chertoff, a lawyer and former prosecutor from New Jersey who would go on to become George W. Bush's secretary of homeland security, to lead the investigative team. In 1995, Dave became a part of the Senate team, along with some of the most dogged investigators you could put together. There was Alice Fisher, who would later become head of the criminal division at DOJ and was in the command center on 9/11, and John Yoo, who became the deputy assistant attorney general and was one of the creators of the rendition program during the Bush administration. These guys were heavyweights; if they were coming after you, you'd know it.

In the swamp, however, political operatives were just as mean and nasty—the precursor of what we call the Deep State today—intent on protecting their establishment candidate, Bill Clinton, at any cost. James Carville, George Stephanopoulos, Paul Begala, and Lanny Davis—the four horsemen of the Clinton cabal—are a few who come to mind. Every morning Dave would wake up ready for a brawl with one or all of those guys. Whenever he uncovered a piece of evidence, they'd have a team prepared to shut him down and discredit it. The tactics weren't unlike the ones Bill would later use to cover up his affairs with women. These guys were merciless, and they operated on the edge. And Hillary was no better.

In recent months, some of them have tried to convince the country of Donald Trump's illegitimacy as president. Google the name of any of today's Democrat operatives and you'll find their anti-Trump speeches, op-eds, and policy papers.

Even for the team Dave was on back in the day, the Whitewater investigation was tough—especially considering the obstruction they were experiencing from the Clinton White House. The land deal itself included boxes full of contracts, deeds, bank records, and other documents. If we were going to get deep enough into it to make a map of exactly what went wrong, the committee would need someone who could go over the numbers and contracts looking for any impropriety or mistakes. We needed a team to do a deep dive on these financial records, what some call "forensic accounting."

One of the people whom Chertoff hired was a long-limbed, lanky lawyer from the University of Chicago named James Comey. As he does now, Comey back then had a tight smile, spoke in crisp, polished sentences, and was unfailingly polite at all times. For a short time, Dave was on the team with Comey. The young, tall lawyer got his work done and rarely complained about anything. Dave never even asked what Comey's political leanings were—he might have voted for Bill Clinton for all he knew (although Comey maintains he's been a Republican for years).

With Comey's help, the team uncovered a massive amount of evidence to suggest that Bill and Hillary had been involved in the crooked land deal, and despite unprecedented obstruction from the White House, the team had managed to track down enough evidence to make a compelling argument, long before the whole thing became overshadowed by the Monica Lewinsky scandal. The committee conducted hundreds of depositions and swore in dozens of witnesses for public hearings.

Then, one day, Comey stopped showing up. If it had been anyone else, Dave might not have noticed the absence at all. But at his height, James Comey is hard to miss. Dave figured he probably headed off to a long career of investigating stock fraud and tax cheats.

Later on someone told Dave that Comey had become uncomfortable with the work the team was doing. The hearings had become openly partisan and people assumed Comey didn't want to be involved. However, Comey had also experienced a terrible personal tragedy around that time—his infant son passed away, an experience that no parent should ever have to go through. Whatever the reason, Comey left silently, virtually in the night, without a trace to somewhere far away from the nitty-gritty of the Clinton investigations.

Many people would have folded under the pressure that was exerted on the investigative team. With the help of the mainstream media, the Clintons portrayed them as right-wing zealots who'd been given too much power. The propaganda from the media—which had already become a shameless mouthpiece for the Democrat Party—came in a constant barrage on cable shows, major newspapers, and entrenched establishment pundits across the media. Clinton surrogates like Carville and Begala hammered the investigation on TV every day.

As it turned out, the Clintons and the MSM would prevail in this round, but the investigation opened the door to the whole scope of the Clintons' crooked operation. Over the years since, Dave, along with Bannon, Matt Drudge, and others, would continue to uncover Clinton dirt by the dump truck load. They'd vowed they wouldn't stop until the complete, dirty truth about the Arkansas couple was revealed.

As we know, Comey didn't ride off to become some anonymous desk jockey. Instead, he would climb to perhaps the most prestigious job in all of law enforcement— director of the FBI. And yet, somehow even with all of the power and prestige that position holds, it wouldn't be enough for him.

He wanted more. It seems he didn't have a "higher loyalty." He wanted the power to decide who would, and who wouldn't, be the next President of the United States.

Back at Trump Tower, after the briefing with the president-elect ended, Director Comey was walking toward the elevators when Dave spotted him. Dave called out his name and he got ready to shake his hand and reintroduce himself— but that wasn't necessary. Dave figured he would give him one of those good-to-see-ya introductions that included his name, so the FBI director wouldn't be embarrassed about having forgotten it. Comey approached, casting a shadow over him. As Dave was about to remind Comey who he was, the director reached over and shook his hand.

"Hey, Dave!" he said, smiling. "Good to see you."

Dave chatted with Comey for a few seconds, but there wasn't much time, or much really to say. Clapper and Brennan had already made their way down the elevators, apparently intent on leaving Trump Tower as quickly as possible. Dave and Comey exchanged pleasantries and parted ways.

In the months that followed, Dave would go on to call Comey "the last Boy Scout," sometimes on television. Even when it began to look like Comey was playing both sides, Dave gave him the benefit of the doubt. Comey had always seemed to him like a principled guy. He figured he was a straight shooter, one of the few who couldn't be compromised and wouldn't display their partisan leanings in a way that was harmful to anyone. To Dave, he was the same gangly lawyer he'd worked with on the Whitewater investigation.

But Dave hadn't yet seen the real Comey—the one who for political reasons refused to prosecute Hillary Clinton, the man who, out of vanity and misplaced egotism, would paint himself as the noble hero and never apologize for what he'd done. The man who would break the law himself by leaking secret documents to a professor with explicit instructions to leak them to the press. The man who perjured himself in front of Congress on multiple occasions.

Dave also hadn't seen the slim, thirty-five-page file that Comey brought with him that morning and was trying hard to keep out of sight of cameras and prying eyes. So, Dave had no idea the damage the file would inflict on the country and Donald Trump's presidency.

With that, though none of us knew it at the time, the battle lines were drawn. That meeting was the first shot fired in a war between our populist, nationalist campaign and the forces that wanted to overturn the results of the 2016 presidential election.

Clapper and Brennan had gone back down in the elevator by the time Comey came out of the conference room, a SCIF, actually, or Sensitive Compartmented

Information Facility. This was a room that took three days to build for the president-elect in Trump Tower, during which time the U.S. Secret Service guarded the facility in order to make sure it was completely secure. A SCIF is a U.S. Department of Defense term for a secure room. It can be a room or data center that guards against electronic surveillance and suppresses data leakage of sensitive security and military information. After Comey left, Dave went back into his office and the president-elect went up to the twenty-sixth floor.

What we didn't know then was that the dossier Comey told the president-elect about had been compiled by a British intelligence officer—someone who knew Russia well and who had worked with the FBI—according to Comey.

The events the dossier described were ridiculous. There were details of meetings that never happened, people Trump had never met—even, in some cases, people who didn't exist. But the most salient detail of all—the one we knew the media would grab and run with as soon as they got hold of the thing—was an absurd, unverified, and unsourced tale about some prostitutes and a hotel room where Barack Obama had once slept.

Now, when something as ridiculous as that comes across your desk, there isn't much you can do other than laugh. As Dave remembers, he and Bannon did some locker room material on it; they may have called Corey to tell him one of the jokes.

But then things got serious.

"This is way outside protocol," Bannon said. "This was given to the president-elect in an official briefing and it doesn't have any kind of stamp of approval on it. This wasn't supposed to be in the meeting."

According to people we've spoken with since, even bringing that dossier into a meeting with a president-elect went against standard operating procedures and rules of intelligence. Anything that is presented in one of those briefings goes through a detailed vetting process, then becomes part of the historical record. It is done that way so we can understand how and why presidents make the decisions they make, and understand what information they had available to them at the time. It is how future historians will determine, for example, why Barack Obama decided to expel all those Russian diplomats from the country, or if he had indeed been given a presentation.

But this dossier wasn't verified material. It should have stayed in a drawer at the FBI with all the other tinfoil hat stuff they get over the course of a year. It wasn't on the level, and Comey very likely would have known that.

But he wanted it leaked, and there was no way for him to do it securely. The dossier had been an open secret among journalists for months, but no organization would publish it because the material was unverified. Even the Fake News wouldn't touch it.

So Comey improvised.

By bringing that folder into his briefing with Trump, Comey transformed the dossier from unverified fiction to "a document that was presented to the president-elect in a private briefing with intelligence agencies." Fake News organizations could now make it sound like an essential piece of information.

Comey had given the fake dossier legitimacy, and the Fake News license to print the whole thing, which *BuzzFeed* did a day later. He admitted he did this in his own memos, writing that CNN was waiting for a "news hook" to publish the trash. Comey had handed them the hook. Within hours, the news was all over the place. Talk show hosts were having a field day with the golden-shower material and journalists were hard at work trying to prove that all the fake meetings had actually occurred. The Russia investigation now had enough juice to run as long as the Democrats could stand it—and it put them one step closer to bringing down the president-elect, which had been their goal since the morning after the election.

Neither of us have ever seen the fake dossier. Anyone who has or was involved in creating this fake document earns themselves a one-way ticket to Robert Mueller–ville.

Still, we needed to know why the dossier was so important, and how it all started.

CHAPTER 4

PHONY DOSSIER

WE HAVE COME TO REALIZE that the intricacies of the lies in the Steele dossier were much more complex than any of us could have imagined. The pieces that were potentially at least half-credible have been proven totally false, and the parts we thought were just innocent mistakes have been revealed to be malicious, coordinated attacks. In some sense, this collection of documents was the beginning of the intelligence community's war on Donald Trump.

Without it, there would be no Russia investigation. Period.

The story goes like this: seven months before the 2016 election, a sleazy political operative and a Washington lawyer walked into a room. We know that sounds like the first line of a joke, but by the end, we promise you won't be laughing.

According to investigators on Capitol Hill, we're now able to say for certain that this meeting, which actually occurred in April 2016, was the first real step taken by the enemies of the president in their ongoing war against Donald J. Trump. What began as a simple, immoral request for dirt on the candidate ended in the wholesale appropriation of America's intelligence agencies by the Democrats, for use against their political opponents—something that turned out to be the biggest scam of the century.

The lawyer was a man named Marc Elias, an expert on the darker sides of campaigns and elections. He had arranged the meeting on behalf of his boss, Hillary Rodham Clinton. Elias' law firm, Perkins Coie, was on retainer for the Clinton campaign and would be paid millions of dollars by the Clinton campaign, mostly in lump sums that weren't itemized—almost as if they were trying to hide something.

Elias was there to meet with Glenn Simpson, who was legendary around the Beltway for a "research" firm he had founded called Fusion GPS. When you were looking for dirt on a political candidate—especially if that candidate was a Republican—and you didn't care much about the sources and methods, Glenn Simpson was your man. Scruffy, always with his shirttails out, Simpson had a reputation for hiring his work out to foreign sources, keeping quiet about expenses, and delivering the most salacious, career-ending details possible.

Even Bossie, who had a working relationship with Glenn Simpson for a few years in the 1990s when Simpson was a reporter at the *Wall Street Journal*, could never have guessed the depths to which the guy was about to sink.

When Dave was on the Whitewater investigation, he would sometimes share a story or a document with Simpson, who was known as a good investigative reporter. In those days, the glut of information that was coming from the investigations into the Clintons was like candy for investigative reporters, and Simpson was one of the best. Dave provided documentary evidence to Simpson and in turn Simpson would break news in the *Journal*. Simpson was so good at digging for information, in fact, that in the late 1990s he left journalism for good and founded his first opposition research firm in Washington, D.C. The new gig provided all the pleasure of digging up dirt but released him from all the strictures of accountability. The new firm wasn't Fusion GPS, but a smaller outfit called SNS Global LLC, which he had started with a two-time Pulitzer Prize–winning reporter from the *Washington Post*.

Within a year and a half of working with Glenn Simpson, the former *Post* reporter, Susan Schmidt, parted ways with him. Now that Schmidt was out of the picture, Simpson doubled down on his dirty tactics, founding Fusion GPS in 2011. This firm was everything that he'd always wanted his company to be: secretive, far-reaching, and unafraid to roll around in the dirt. Clients came to him for sordid details of their opponents' lives, and frequently came away satisfied. There's no telling how many up-and-coming politicians you've probably never heard of because of Simpson's work. By the time the 2016 election came around, Simpson's reputation preceded him.

When he met with Marc Elias at the headquarters of Fusion GPS, they made a rough plan for securing opposition research on Donald Trump, the most feared Republican candidate since Reagan. Knowing what we know about this process—having gotten pretty deep into opposition research ourselves—we can assume that they probably agreed to go after Trump on his businesses, and the many relationships he had forged with businessmen in foreign countries. As luck would have it, Simpson had already done a little work on this front. During the primary elections, a conservative website (funded by establishment billionaire Paul Singer), the *Free Beacon*, had come to him in search of the same kind of information Marc Elias and Clinton were now looking for. He had gotten started quickly but hadn't found much on his own. Then, once Donald Trump became the Republican nominee, the conservative website stopped paying, not wanting to take shots at the head of their own party.

But the business angle was still a good one. When you're dealing with a guy who's got as much money and success as Donald Trump does, and as many varied interests in different countries around the world, it isn't very hard to try to make him look bad somehow. You have to figure with all those hotels, all those restaurants, all those people who'd worked at his casinos, there had to be at least one person who'd done something bad that could be traced back to Trump. Luckily, they would stay on this trail for a long time and find nothing, but it didn't matter very much to them. When you're dead set on sliming someone the way they were on Donald Trump, you can make bad things appear out of thin air, twisting rumors into facts, and biased testimony into disinterested observation. This, as we now know, is exactly what Glenn Simpson would do.

We can't be sure what Simpson and Marc Elias actually agreed to during the meeting, or whether Simpson discussed his methods and staff while they were talking. All we know is what happened in the months that followed—and how much cash the Clinton campaign shelled out for Simpson's work. The numbers are staggering, even for a presidential campaign. Between May and November 2016, the Clinton campaign paid Perkins Coie, the law firm of Marc Elias, $12.4 million, more than $1 million of which went directly to Glenn Simpson and Fusion GPS for "research."

On the bank records that were eventually obtained by Republicans in Congress—which Fusion would fight like mad to keep them from getting—the charges were never enumerated specifically, but the timing makes the purpose of the payments clear. Hillary Clinton and her campaign were directly engaged in paying a firm to dig up dirt on Donald Trump and his associates. During most campaigns, this would be completely normal. People do it all the time. What's alarming is the manner in which Glenn Simpson went about getting this information, and then what he and the U.S. intelligence community did with it afterward.

That's when desperate tactics were put in play.

Simpson's first move was to decide exactly where he was going to look for dirt. He knew they would focus on Trump's business dealings but wasn't sure exactly where to look. After all, the man had real estate holdings all over the world and there was no way Simpson's humble little opposition shop could have combed through all the records in time to have them influence the election. For Simpson, however, the process of narrowing down his search wasn't very difficult. He knew exactly where he wanted to look, and where he had the best chance of finding some Fake News.

That place was Mother Russia.

According to testimony that he would later give about his actions that summer, Glenn Simpson was obsessed with Russian banking and its connection to organized crime and New York real estate and not only as an interested observer. He had once worked for a Russian company implicated in a money-laundering scheme that had ties to the Kremlin. He knew that when you ran a business in Russia, it was a near certainty that, whether they were crooked oligarchs or small-time, tracksuit-wearing mobsters, at least a few bad hombres would be circling like buzzards around it. His first move—after the first check from Marc Elias had cleared, of course—was to assemble a team. To do this, he flipped through his Rolodex and came up with, perhaps, the perfect co-conspirator.

Nellie Ohr was an expert in cybersecurity, equally as obsessed with Russia as Simpson was. She had graduated from Harvard University with a degree in history and Russian literature and went on to obtain a PhD in history from Stanford. She was fluent in Russian and even lived in the Soviet Union when she was working on her doctorate. She wrote scholarly articles about the history of the Soviet Union and taught at Vassar College. Ohr's entrance into cybersecurity came with a politically connected firm called Accenture, famous for rescuing the crashed Obamacare website. In other words, she had all the tools Simpson needed to give the appearance of substance to his "research" on Mr. Trump.

She is also the wife of Bruce Ohr, who was an assistant deputy attorney general, or fourth in line from the top, in Obama's Department of Justice, which, at least on the surface, would seem like a convenient little arrangement for a conspiracy. Bruce Ohr never reported the fact that his wife was working for Fusion GPS, or that she got paid $45,000 for her work on the dossier, to his bosses at the Department of Justice, which puts him in violation of several well-established regulations of our government.

Once Simpson had hired Nellie Ohr, they began their opposition research on Donald Trump. Her husband, Bruce, was kept in the loop of their progress. This was important because Bruce reported to Sally Yates, the deputy attorney general. See how nice and cozy everything was?

Ohr and Fusion found out that the task of finding dirt on Donald Trump was a lot harder than they first believed. Everything they looked into was clean as a whistle. Even a notoriously shady opposition research firm can only invent so much. In fact, after a great deal of digging into Trump's financial history, they gave up and took a different direction.

That new direction led to the now-infamous Christopher Steele.

Steele was a former spy from across the Atlantic Ocean who allegedly knew how to get information. American intelligence agencies had used him as a confidential source in the past, and so had Glenn Simpson. Word around Washington, apparently, was that he could dip into his Rolodex full of Russian oligarchs and come up with just about any information you were looking for.

Steele had worked for decades as an agent of MI6, Britain's foreign intelligence service, including a few years in the 1990s as the head of the agency's "Russia desk." He spent most of his life on the ground in Russia, back when it was still called the Soviet Union, trying to collect intelligence about things that pertained to Britain's national security. Think of his job as writing a really long research paper that goes on for thirty years.

For the most part, his work involved little more than interviews and phone calls. Steele had graduated from Cambridge University, one of the top colleges in the world— and, as it would turn out, a spy factory—and joined MI6 right out of school, lured in by the prospect of travel and meeting interesting people. His work as a "spy" was more about research than it was killing bad guys. He would get information, try to track its source, and then present it in dull folders and dull presentations.

Fusion GPS hired Steele in June 2016, and he got to work. From the looks of it, he had gotten a little bored with his time behind a desk and started chasing all the sordid details he could think of. Hookers, backroom deals, mob stuff. It was almost as if he was trying to keep himself relevant in the Russian underworld. Looking back on his career, this is understandable. Steele only spent three years undercover in Moscow, from 1990 to 1993. It was during that time the Soviet Union collapsed, as did the Cold War spy business. Like a high school sports hero, Steele had three years of glory and spent the rest of his life trying to recapture them.

According to early accounts about the dossier, he traveled to Russia and interviewed some sources he'd developed over the course of his career, talking about Trump and anyone who had ever worked with him. His interviewees—again, allegedly—included a hotel clerk, an alleged spy, and a few bankers Trump was supposed to have worked with or seen during a visit to Russia. From them, as the story goes, Steele found out the stories of the famous "pee tape," a real estate deal Trump had cut in the 1980s, and a few stories about rat lawyer Michael Cohen visiting Prague—something he had allegedly done three times on behalf of Donald Trump (which we now know not to be true). According to Cohen, he never set foot in Prague and Steele never set foot in Russia during his "research" for the document. Instead, he did most of his "investigating" on the phone. Records would later confirm that he hadn't even been back to Russia since 2009, when he went there on a business trip. He had good reason for not traveling to Russia. He was considered "an enemy of Mother Russia by Putin's government."

What he couldn't get on the phone, Steele got from a small community of expatriated Russians living in London. These were people who had fled their home country after the dissolution of the Soviet Union, angry about the way the Putin government was running things. In more than one sense, this meant that the people Steele used to collect his information had just as much reason to be angry at Russia as he did. When a British spy came knocking to ask if Trump had done anything wrong with Russia, they were very happy to tell him whatever crazy anti-Russia lies the guy wanted to hear. From all angles, the dossier was constructed by angry, misguided people, using false information that came from those same people.

It's a perfect case study in Trump Derangement Syndrome, which seems to have found its way over the Atlantic Ocean between May and July 2016. By the time Steele's dossier made it back to the shores of the United States, TDS had reached pandemic levels. Everyone from reporters and columnists to political junkies and rogue agents at the FBI was looking for reasons to hate Donald Trump even more than they already did.

The dossier was about to give them exactly the reason they'd been looking for.

Even though Steele probably spent most of the investigation in crested slippers and a smoking jacket in the parlor of his London flat with his three cats (one of which, it is said, had a penchant for peeing on his bed), he did manage to give Simpson his money's worth. Not that the information was true, of course. But, then again, it didn't have to be true, it just had to be salacious. You can't get much more salacious than the Steele dossier.

With the imagination of a paperback spy novelist, and an affinity for stories about weird sex, Steele assembled a tale of lurid encounters and secret meetings between campaign officials and spies, all supposedly orchestrated at the highest reaches of the Russian government. It's no surprise, given the anti-Putin and anti-Trump bias of Steele's sources, or the hatred of Donald Trump he had displayed repeatedly during the campaign.

No doubt Glenn Simpson was thrilled when he received the first packet of the dossier, hand delivered by courier. Information like that comes around only once every few years. Like most failed fiction authors, however, he found that writing the story was the easy part. Getting someone to buy the work was another thing altogether.

When people hear the word "dossier," they tend to think it sounds very official and international. But what it actually looked like was a loosely connected packet of political opposition research memos, written by Christopher Steele from the comfort of his office and shipped piecemeal to Fusion GPS between June and December 2016.

Though Simpson was overjoyed, the information the dossier contained was so outrageous, even the Clinton campaign didn't want to use it at first. The Clinton campaign and the DNC decided to hide it away for the summer, hoping they would be able to beat Donald Trump on their own.

Glenn Simpson and Christopher Steele, however, weren't about to let it sit and collect dust. In July 2016, Steele met with FBI contacts in Europe and briefed them on what he'd already collected. He also met with some of his old compatriots from British intelligence. Later that month he started leaking his tale to journalists, instructing them the information was off the record. Obviously, he was seeding the story, hoping some news organization would pour Miracle-Gro on it. Any good reporter would have set the thing on fire and moved on to something else. At first, most did.

By September, Simpson and Steele dropped all pretense of secrecy. Simpson set up meetings with media outlets in Manhattan, practically begging them to publish the dirty details of their dossier. They found no takers.

"We, like others, investigated the allegations and haven't corroborated them, and we felt we're not in the business of publishing things we can't stand by," said Dean Baquet, executive editor for the *New York Times*. The *Times*, however, was only one stop on what would become a very long tour for the two men, a trek that included meeting national security reporters in Washington, D.C.

Apparently, the veracity of the allegations in Steele's report—which Simpson never attempted to verify, in either a personal or a professional capacity—didn't matter much to either of them. What mattered was taking down Donald Trump, a man for whom both men had expressed anger and scorn in the months leading up to the election. Simpson boldly admitted his disdain for Trump when he was interviewed by the Senate.

In later depositions and investigations, Glenn Simpson's lack of concern about whether or not the information in that dossier was true became public. He believed that the kind of information contained within the dossier was actually beyond verification, whatever that means. "By its very nature," he told the Senate committee, "the question of whether something is accurate isn't really asked."

Though every media outlet that Simpson and Steele met with initially said no, these guys, peddling their "beyond verification" garbage, weren't about to give up.

The Fake News, they knew, was not their only play.

Nellie Ohr's husband, Bruce, is a Harvard-educated lawyer who worked as a federal prosecutor in Manhattan in the 1990s. One of the cases he caught back then was the prosecution of a drug gangster from the Washington Heights section of Manhattan, which at that time was like headquarters for New York City's crack cocaine business.

Ohr won the case (he was actually one of a team of pros-ecutors) and the drug dealer was convicted of murdering seven of his rivals and received the sentence of life with-out parole. The reason this case is important to Ohr's story is what happened after. The *New York Times* covered the case extensively, a series of stories that included a long pro-file of the dealer and Ohr's successful trial. Getting good notices in the Fake News goes a long way to help a fed-eral prosecutor's career. It did for Ohr. Soon after, he was snatched away by the Justice Department in Washington (Main Justice), where he was soon put in charge of the agency's Organized Crime Drug Enforcement Task Forces (OCDETF). Ohr's relationship with "the paper of record" may explain his alleged actions in the months preceding the 2016 presidential election. A Peter Strzok text from October 7, 2016, read: "Jesus. More BO leaks in the NYT."

The relationship between Ohr and Steele, however, is still somewhat of a mystery. According to published reports, they knew each other since 2007 and had met at least three times leading up to the 2016 presidential campaign.

But it was a meeting sometime in August 2016 that is the most curious. It was then, when the dossier was com-plete and every credible news agency had passed on it, that Glenn Simpson and Christopher Steele (we don't know exactly when, because Simpson, who was inconsistent, failed to disclose the meeting when he testified under oath before the Senate) both met with Ohr in an undisclosed location. There's little doubt, seeing as his wife worked on the project for Fusion GPS, that Ohr already knew a great deal about the story that Simpson and Steele must have been peddling.

It was after that meeting that the dossier grew wings. Within days it was flying around at the highest levels of the American government—and people were actually taking it seriously. Evidently, when it came to disinformation against Donald Trump, the chiefs of federal intelligence agencies and law enforcement stopped paying attention to basic facts. All that seemed to matter was that they had opposition ammunition on Donald Trump, their sworn enemy, which finally gave them a chance to take a shot at him. The details in the dossier—if they were true, which they weren't—were certainly enough to warrant a federal investigation. After all, according to this piece of paper, a candidate for president of the United States had been groomed as an asset of the Russian secret service! How could you not investigate that?

As if the resources of the FBI weren't enough, there's more. According to a footnote in the House intelligence report on Russian interference in the 2016 election, an investment group led by Clinton funder George Soros and other wealthy donors provided a war chest of $50 million to track down and verify the dossier's more salacious details. The information reviewed by the committee came from leaked texts and other correspondence between Senator Mark Warner (D-VA) and a registered foreign agent for a Russian aluminum oligarch. According to the *Federalist* magazine, those documents describe an ex-FBI agent named Daniel J. Jones, who was conducting an investigation to "retroactively validate a series of salacious and unverified memos produced by Christopher Steele, a former British intelligence agent, and Fusion GPS." Along with working for the FBI, Jones was a former staffer for Democrat senator Dianne Feinstein.

Had the information in the dossier been accurate, the actions that the FBI, CIA, and DOJ took next would have been completely legal. In fact, they would have been downright patriotic. But as we know, none of it was true. Even $50 million couldn't prove them true. All any of them had to do was make a few phone calls to find that out. But they didn't.

CHAPTER 5

DIGGING DIRT

IN MARCH 2016, at a dark bar in London not far from the offices of Christopher Steele, a campaign volunteer named George Papadopoulos had a few too many drinks with an Australian diplomat. What happened next would implicate both men in the Russia hoax for good, and land one of them in a jail cell for fourteen days.

Late into the night, Papadopoulos divulged some unfounded gossip. According to rumors he had picked up from a shady Maltese professor named Joseph Mifsud, whom he'd met on a recent trip to Russia, the Russian government was compiling a large volume of unflattering information on Hillary Clinton, which included, by the professor's estimation, "thousands of emails." Papadopoulos never speculated to the diplomat, whose name was Alexander Downer, as to where those emails may have come from, or how the Russian government planned on using them. He had no way of knowing that information.

Still, Papadopoulos thought that the cache of emails was big news, and in a momentary lapse of judgment, he shared it with his drinking buddy.

All night, the circumstances of the meeting had seemed suspicious. After all, diplomats at Downer's level rarely met with people as low on the totem pole as Papadopoulos, and the circumstances that had brought them together were very odd. In the days before being "lured" into the meeting with Downer, Papadopoulos remembers being introduced to an Israeli diplomat who hated Trump. This Israeli, whose name was Christian Cantor, then connected Papadopoulos to his "girlfriend," who was from Australia and worked closely with Downer. It all happened very fast. The meeting for drinks, as Papadopoulos would later phrase it, seemed "very controlled" the whole time.

But that wouldn't become clear in his mind until later. At the time of the meeting, Papadopoulos' quick slip about the Russian emails must have sounded like an unverified rumor, coming from a young man who wanted to impress a top diplomat. We should also emphasize that though Papadopoulos was a campaign volunteer, he traveled to London on his own. This trip had nothing to do with, nor was it sanctioned by, the Trump campaign. He sat in on one organizational meeting early in the campaign where there was no substantive discussions about policy. To the best of our knowledge, he never came to the campaign office and was never seen again by anyone in a senior leadership capacity. But there seemed to be someone watching him that night—someone in Australian intelligence, which somehow got a full record of the conversation in the days to come. This leads us to believe that this meeting, which has been widely reported as an accidental slip of the tongue that Alexander Downer felt he had to report out of adherence to process, was actually a setup by the global intelligence community. It was the piece of evidence they'd been looking for to connect the Trump campaign with Russia, and one they would soon share with the FBI once they had a believable pretext for doing so.

In the meantime, the FBI wanted to collect more information on possible ties between Russia and the Trump campaign. Due to the constitutional protections afforded to American citizens, this would require a court order.

In the United States, when intelligence agencies like the National Security Agency (NSA) and the FBI want to spy on people, they have to make a series of formal requests. This is supposed to ensure that their power doesn't go unchecked, and that U.S. citizens aren't unfairly targeted by the government the way they were in the days of J. Edgar Hoover's FBI. The people who decide this are part of what's called the Foreign Intelligence Surveillance Court, or FISC. The judges in this court are typically allowed to preside over their benches in secret, and they're supposed to have a very high standard of evidence for granting warrants.

To get permission to spy on someone, the intelligence agency in question needs to present proof that that person is probably guilty of a crime. In most cases, this proof takes the form of photographs, phone records, or information and documents from a prior investigation. If the FBI were investigating a terrorist cell, for example, and they caught someone collaborating with them, they could then apply for a warrant against that person and probably get it. All that would be necessary are photographs or recorded tapes of the person collaborating with terrorists.

Needless to say, that kind of proof isn't always easy to get, and intelligence agencies have to make sure they don't rely on shoddy research. What's usually forbidden, except in extreme circumstances, is conducting surveillance on American citizens, which violates, among other things, the Fourth Amendment of the Constitution. If the DOJ tries that in court, the application is usually denied. But there are ways, as anyone in the FBI and DOJ knows very well, of bending the rules when circumstances require it. Members of the intelligence community often ask for warrants to surveil certain buildings or computers, knowing that certain American citizens might be around, and that their conversations might be picked up "by accident." This is called "incidental collection," and it's very easy to conceal. Incidental collection happens when someone who is under surveillance gets in touch with someone else who is not. By law, all communications that occur during that conversation are subject to surveillance, even what is said from the side of the person who isn't under surveillance. This happens under most standard surveillance programs, whether someone is being watched under a FISA order or not.

This is why, in June 2016—on a day that still hasn't been revealed—one of Barack Hussein Obama's DOJ line attorneys, who was there on behalf of Sally Yates, traveled to the E. Barrett Prettyman Courthouse in Washington, D.C., where they joined about a dozen other lawyers from the CIA, DOJ, FBI, the DNI, and the NSA. Clapper, Comey, and Brennan weren't there. They instead sent their lawyers, who represented their agencies at FISA hearings.

Sources say the attorney carried an application for a warrant that would effectively allow the U.S. intelligence community to monitor the communications of several members of the Trump campaign—one of them being Carter Page.

Allegedly, the warrant pertained to the connection between a Russian bank and some computers in Trump Tower, along with other, more broad activities of Russian banks in general. This is how they hid the information. The intelligence collected from these computers would be "a matter of national security," they said, and should be acted upon immediately. What they didn't say was that they had very little proof of any connection between the Trump campaign and this Russian bank. They wanted to listen in to the conversations of anyone coming in and out of Trump Tower, probably in the hope that they'd be able to use what they heard to cook up some kind of crime.

When the judge—whose name, like the date of the hearing, still hasn't been revealed to the public—read the warrant, he was repulsed. Apparently, according to what the various departments had written, the warrant made it seem as if the Justice Department was applying for permission to spy on American citizens, who, to make matters worse, were members of an opposing political party. He even left the bench to do a conference call with other FISA judges, who displayed similar surprise. In the intelligence community, the practice of seeking a warrant for something in the hope that you'll be able to catch the people "around" that thing in a crime—especially when the thing in question resides inside the United States— is called spying for "incidental collection," and it's illegal. The law grants these agencies the right to conduct surveillance on foreign targets only; that's what the *F* in *FISA* means—foreign!

Despite an effort by the DOJ line attorney and a dozen other lawyers in the room, the judge denied the application for a warrant. This happens to only two out of every hundred applications that come before the FISA court, and it's reserved only for requests that are blatantly illegal demonstrating how poorly the application by the DOJ was written. The standard for evidence that comes before the FISA court, as we know, is shockingly low, and has been for years. But it's been allowed to remain that way largely because no one's allowed to know how FISA warrants are either granted or denied.

That's the advantage of running a secret court.

But the judge left the door open. He told the DOJ attorney and the other lawyers to redraft the application in a way that looked less suspicious, then try again. When you're dealing with the secret courts of the Deep State, it doesn't matter which side of the bench you're on; everyone's on the same dark, secret team in the end.

Drafting another warrant, however, would take some time. The Obama Justice Department needed to scrub the document of any suggestion that it was trying to use the FISA courts to spy on their political rivals, and they needed to get some evidence that seemed a little more credible. This, they knew, would be almost impossible. There was no evidence that any of the people they had been hoping to spy on had any illegal contacts with Russia—at least no real evidence.

Luckily, shortly after the FBI's first FISA warrant was rejected, Christopher Steele contacted the bureau and asked for a meeting. He had been trying to sell his phony dossier to media outlets for months, and no one was taking the bait. The American intelligence community—who, he must have thought, would believe anything—were his last hope for getting the thing out into the world. Proving him correct, the FBI took the meeting and allowed him to come to their headquarters for a briefing.

This is how, only one day after James Comey cleared Hillary Clinton of all blame for her email scandal—and before anyone knew that there were another 600,000 waiting on the laptop of Anthony Weiner—special agents at the FBI ended up in a meeting with Christopher Steele, the author of the phony dossier. As we mentioned before, the FBI had used Steele as a source in the past, so the agency and the foreign agent had a good working relationship, with "working" being the operative word. Steele had been on the FBI payroll for years. During the meeting, the FBI got more information on the infamous dossier. Unlike the Fake News, which had to report to its viewers and maintain some level of public trust, amazingly, the FBI fully accepted every premise of the dossier without a second thought. Anyone at the FBI offices with access to Google could have disproved many of its claims in just a few minutes. But no one did.

Soon after meeting with Steele, the FBI started doing exploratory research into the Trump campaign and Russia, hoping they would gather enough evidence to begin an investigation.

We should say right away that many of the actions taken by the FBI during July 2016 raise various questions about ethics and legality. Even looking into the Trump campaign based on nothing but a rumor goes against the policy of the bureau. It's widely accepted that the FBI is only supposed to investigate crimes when there is credible evidence that

something is wrong. According to the bureau's own manual, an investigation cannot begin unless a special agent
has identified "a particular crime or a threatened crime."
In other words, there needs to be credible evidence that a
crime will be committed if the FBI does not act, and that
evidence needs to be based on something substantial and,
it should go without saying, not motivated by politics.

Obviously, that isn't what happened here. On the day
they began investigating the Trump campaign's supposed
collusion with Russia, the only evidence in front of the
bureau was a dossier that had been paid for by Hillary
Clinton and the DNC, then vetted by exactly no one. They
were investigating a crime before a crime had been committed and doing it because they feared a politician they dis-
agreed with might gain power. It was the ultimate example
of an intelligence agency looking for a crime where there
was nothing to be found.

To dig up some dirt, the FBI called on another one of its
old sources—one who worked at the university where
Christopher Steele was educated and lived part-time in
London. Like Steele, he had done some investigative work
for the FBI in the past, so the bureau already had him on
the payroll.

His name was Stefan Halper, and his hatred of people
in the orbit of Donald Trump was deep.

In July 2016, two years after the dinner with Michael
Flynn, and while James Comey and the FBI were meeting
with Christopher Steele about a dossier, Stefan Halper was
spending less and less time around his offices at Cambridge

University. Donald Trump was the Republican nominee for the presidency of the United States, and Michael Flynn— the man Halper and his spy buddies had been so put off by two years earlier—was one of Trump's key campaign surrogates. In Halper's mind, Flynn, who had been compromised by Russian spies, was now a key advisor to the Republican nominee.

This must have terrified him.

In many ways, according to sources, Halper saw the Cold War as never having ended. He became obsessed with living out his James Bond fantasies, even as he approached his late sixties. This is evident not only in the jobs he took for American intelligence services but also the students he recruited and trained. According to his colleagues at Magdalen College, the branch of Cambridge University where he was a dean, Halper had always had a fondness for young recruits. Records show that he usually kept students awake late into the night with tales of his escapades in the United States, letting them ask questions in his office at Cambridge until they couldn't think of any more. Conflicts with Russia often figured prominently in these tales, and it was always framed as a battle between good and evil.

He also told them stories about his father-in-law, the notorious CIA agent Ray Cline, whose daughter Halper had married in the early 1970s. In the Kennedy administration, Cline was the agent assigned to oversee relations with the Soviet Union during the Cuban Missile Crisis. He was the one who actually looked at the black-and-white photographs of missiles and warned John F. Kennedy about what exactly the Russians were shipping into Cuba. This, we would imagine, only fueled Halper's obsession with

Moscow and its ongoing "war" with the West. In his mind, Halper was the rogue secret agent—a job he never got to do in real life, given that he was consigned to a desk and a drab office for most of his working life—and Russia was the eternal enemy, waging a never-ending war on Britain and the United States. Much like Richard Dearlove and his real-spy friends, Halper had never been able to let go of Russia. He was obsessed, likely looking for a way to get in on the action.

Then, in June 2016, the FBI gave him the opportunity.

The FBI had just had its broad-scope attempt at the FISA warrant rejected. They needed more evidence to tap Carter Page's wires but didn't just want to sit on their hands in the meantime. So, someone in the FBI's office suggested hiring Stefan Halper to do a little old-school reconnaissance on Carter Page, Michael Flynn, and George Papadopoulos. For that, they didn't need a warrant.

Over the course of that summer, Stefan Halper lured three members of the campaign to England and conducted covert interviews with them. He started by inviting Page to a seminar at Cambridge, just the way he'd done with Flynn in 2014, and conducting an interview with him about the Russians. They continued to talk over email, but nothing much came of their interactions.

Strike one.

Sam Clovis, a college professor who gave the president some strategic advice during the campaign, was next. They had coffee in England, but couldn't provide him with anything either. Strike two. Clovis did, however, lead Halper to Papadopoulos, the guy who'd been caught in a bar blabbering about some "dirt" that the Russians supposedly had on Hillary Clinton.

Halper and Papadopoulos met at a bar in London after Halper had lured him in by offering him three thousand dollars to write a paper for him. The ploy also included a female assistant, who stuck around after Halper left, possibly for an encounter. When Papadopoulos denied that he knew about any Russian interference efforts, Halper got angry and gave up the investigation.

He continued to speak with all three sources but never found any useful information for the FBI. Of course, this didn't stop the government from paying more than $300,000 for his efforts. Unfortunately for the Deep State, however, Stefan Halper quickly became irrelevant.

It was around this time that the press got its fangs into the dossier. The liberal-leaning magazine *Mother Jones* was the first media outlet to report on the phony dossier's existence. They had a source on the inside.

According to our sources, James Baker, the FBI's general counsel, provided documents to David Corn, *Mother Jones'* DC bureau chief. Baker allegedly leaked classified information about the phony dossier to Corn in late October 2016, just before the presidential election. Corn, however, denies this. Not only was Baker James Comey's close buddy and confidant, but also a close friend of Andrew McCabe and Robert Mueller.

Baker was demoted when Christopher Wray took over as FBI chief and left the bureau on May 4, 2018—the same day as Lisa Page, Peter Strzok's girlfriend—went to work for the Brooking Institute, which *Time* magazine once described as "the nation's pre-eminent liberal think tank."

Once all the information comes out, which it invariably will, we believe Baker will be a major player in the conspiracy against President Trump.

In July, timed perfectly with the Democrat National Convention, thousands of emails that had been hacked from computers at the DNC were poured out onto the internet by WikiLeaks. It didn't take a genius to guess that these emails had come from the same hackers we would later hear so much about. This timed release of the emails was nothing, really—just a prank meant to sow discord in the American political system. But the press and the liberals in Congress made it seem like Pearl Harbor.

Apparently the uproar reached Australia, where the intelligence agencies that had been sitting on George Papadopoulos' statements about the Russian government's support for Donald Trump decided to act. In July 2016, they made a call to the FBI and relayed all the information they had on Papadopoulos and what he had told their diplomat in that bar in London—information that the FBI took to mean that the Trump campaign must have been "colluding" with the Russian government. It was all the "proof" Trump's enemies needed to begin their investigation into his campaign.

On July 31, they began Crossfire Hurricane, an operation to investigate the ties of the Trump campaign to Russia. Peter Strzok was in charge. The greatest hoax in American political history was under way.

CHAPTER 6

CROSSFIRE HURRICANE

ON THE DAY THE FBI opened its investigation into Donald Trump, Peter Strzok texted his mistress, FBI attorney Lisa Page. He knew he was going to be named the head of the Crossfire Hurricane team, and he seemed to want Page to share in his excitement.

"Damn," he wrote. "This feels momentous. Because this matters. The other one did, too, but that was to ensure that we didn't F something up. This matters because this MATTERS. So super glad to be on this voyage with you."

The "other one" he was talking about was the Clinton email investigation, which had ended less than a month earlier when James Comey decided to clear Clinton on all charges of wrongdoing. Strzok had been part of a special team at the FBI, code-named "Midyear Exam," that was in charge of looking through Hillary Clinton's emails and trying to find evidence of wrongdoing. He had bungled the process thoroughly, revealing a deep bias for Clinton in the process.

In case you don't remember, the Hillary Clinton email saga began sometime in 2009, when she was preparing to become the top diplomat in the United States. That's also when she set up a private email server in the basement of her home in Chappaqua, New York. Using a private server for official State Department business meant that none of her communications could be reviewed or recorded by people in the government, and gave Clinton full control of the content within. Why she did this is anyone's guess, though a good one would have something to do with the Clinton Foundation, which raised hundreds of millions of dollars from foreign sources over the years. If you were dealing with that kind of dark cash you'd want it to be on a private server, too.

Using a private server to do the logistical business of U.S. secretary of state is bad enough, but Hillary used it for much more than just scheduling. Clinton and her aides at the State Department—including her top aide, Huma Abedin, who had been working with Clinton for almost two decades—discussed classified information using the private email account, which was completely separated from the government's security methods and could therefore be hacked or corrupted at any time. It seems the Clinton team even used cute little code words and euphemisms to refer to the classified information.

The public found out about the secretary of state's private server in 2013 when the website Smoking Gun published Clinton's email address, hdr22@clintonemail.com, and emails Clinton sent from that address to her former aide, Sidney Blumenthal. The world found out that Clinton used the server for government business when the *New York Times* broke the story in March 2015.

At first Clinton leaned on negligence as an excuse. Representatives for her team said that she simply wasn't aware that she wasn't supposed to use her private email account to discuss our nation's most secret information, even though she had taken enough care to disguise that information with funny names and coded language. Luckily for her, she had friends in high places who would look the other way. It's nearly impossible to prove what was in someone's head at the time they committed a crime—as Clinton knew better than anyone—and so the defense of ignorance usually works. In the absence of that "smoking gun" email, which would have revealed that Clinton knew she was breaking the law and went ahead with setting up her private email server anyway, the FBI would never be able to prove intentional wrongdoing.

The FBI wasn't interested in proving wrongdoing, anyway, as evidenced by the decision to "slow-walk" the investigation. Over the course of a year, James Comey, Peter Strzok, and the rest of the Midyear Exam team took their time looking into the emails they had and didn't try very hard to find any additional ones. Sometime after the investigation opened, Clinton and her team promised to provide "all relevant emails" pertaining to the case. Shortly afterward, a team of Hillary Clinton's private lawyers went through every email chain on the server, sorting through the messages for what they promised were merely "duplicates" and "irrelevant materials." If you want proof that the FBI bosses were in Clinton's pocket, look no further than this event. That the lawyers of a subject of investigation were allowed to take a first pass at the evidence that might have incriminated their client is inconceivable.

What Clinton and her lawyers came up with was a package of about 55,000 emails that were either sent or received by Clinton during her tenure as secretary of state. The others, they said, had either been deleted or were duplicates of messages that the FBI already had. For the most part, the FBI took the lawyers at their word and made only weak efforts to look at the materials that had been deleted.

The agency also granted immunity for two top Clinton aides whose computers were used to determine which of Hillary's emails would be turned over to the State Department, an unbelievably biased concession. The aides, Cheryl Mills and Heather Samuelson, were granted immunity under attorney-client privilege. Calling Mills and Samuelson Hillary's lawyers was a stretch. Mills was a former Clinton chief of staff and Samuelson an ex–campaign staffer. Even if the FBI wanted to form a case against Hillary, the immunity given to her "lawyers" would severely hamper any effort. According to reports, the immunity included a "side deal" that demanded the FBI destroy Mills' and Samuelson's computers after they conducted a narrow and cursory search, ensuring no further investigations— the electronic version of "Dead men tell no tales."

The FBI then reviewed the emails from August 2015 through June of 2016, and found several instances in which Clinton and her team had criminally mishandled classified information. Had it been anyone else who did what she had done—with the exact information and circumstances, down to the exact time of day and color of the pantsuit— they would have earned themselves a one-way ticket to federal prison. Clinton, on the other hand, managed to wiggle out of it, using her well-established network of Deep State connections and operatives.

One of those loyalists was Attorney General Loretta Lynch—the woman who was supposed to decide whether to bring charges against Hillary Clinton or not. Lynch was the one who insisted that Comey and the FBI call the Clinton email investigation a "matter," so that it would sound better for the Clinton campaign. The investigation was never called anything other than a "matter" for the rest of the year. Then, on June 27, a week before Comey's public exoneration of Hillary, Attorney General Lynch mysteriously met with Bill Clinton in an airplane cabin on the tarmac of an airport in Phoenix. Bill Clinton told the inspector general that Lynch had invited him onto her plane to "talk about their grandchildren." But the meeting held up air traffic for hours. Hillary's friends at the *New York Times* and the *Washington Post* wrote op-eds decrying the Clinton email scandal as "ridiculous" and a "right-wing conspiracy," not unlike the Whitewater scandals of the 1990s, which had resulted in her husband's impeachment.

Before long, anyone who dared ask about Hillary Clinton's mishandling of thousands of pieces of sensitive government material was labeled a crazy person, a partisan hack, or even both. Even James Comey decided that no charges were to be brought against Hillary.

As you know, the investigation (we're not calling it a "matter") ended on July 5, 2016—which, as you might remember, is the day before Christopher Steele met with agents of the FBI to push the details of his fabricated dossier. James Comey announced that although Hillary Clinton had been "extremely careless" with her mishandling of classified information, and that her actions might have put American lives at risk, they hadn't risen to the level of criminality.

We now know that Peter Strzok, then the agency's number two official in counterintelligence who led the Clinton investigation, changed the language in Comey's first draft of the statement from "grossly negligent" to "extremely careless." Grossly negligent is a criminal act, while extremely careless is a slap on the wrist. Such subtlety may be lost on some, but under scrutiny it was a clear indication of Strzok's nefarious agenda.

The Clinton email investigation never really mattered to Strzok. It was only a prelude to what he really cared about: going after Donald Trump. For months he and his lover, Lisa Page, had been texting back and forth about how disgusted they were at the Republican nominee for president. They had called him all manner of demeaning names, including "douchebag," "loathsome human," and an "idiot." In another exchange in April, Page had expressed joy that Strzok was still at the FBI to "protect the country." Then, on July 24, just after their first attempt at a FISA warrant to spy on the Trump campaign was rejected, Strzok and Page had this damning exchange about a friend of theirs who was a judge. The friend's name was Rudy Contreras, a U.S. district court judge who had just been named to the Foreign Intelligence Surveillance Court, meaning he had the power to grant FISA warrants—even ones that had already been rejected.

Page: Rudy is on the [Foreign Intelligence Surveillance Court]! Did you know that? Just appointed two months ago. . . .

Strzok: I did. We talked about it before and after. I need to get together with him.

Clearly, the lovers, Strzok and Page, were making plans to draft another, cleaner FISA warrant on the Trump campaign and thought they had a friendly judge who would grant their request, even if it was an illegal attempt to conduct "incidental collection." In testimony that he would later give under oath, Peter Strzok would categorically deny that he ever met with Rudy Contreras before drafting another FISA warrant. "At no time," he would say, "did I ever with Judge Contreras think of or in actuality reach out for the purpose of discussing any case or trying to get any decision, provide any information, or otherwise influence him with regard to any investigative matter that I or others were involved with." But his girlfriend, Lisa Page, who would wonder on the text messages whether Contreras should recuse himself—which he didn't—made no such claims. It's entirely possible that she met with Contreras, or other FISA judges whom the love birds didn't talk about over text, in order to make sure that their next FISA warrant would be accepted.

By August, evidence wasn't something they had to worry about. The fake Steele dossier contained all the incriminating material they would need to try to frame people on the Trump campaign that they wanted to spy on. All they had to do was obtain a warrant using the Steele dossier as evidence and try to make it seem more credible than it was. With all the footnotes and fine print involved in drafting a FISA application, this would be very simple. Looking through the dossier, it became clear that one of the easiest targets would be Carter Page, an investment banker who ran an energy firm in New York. Page had lived in Moscow for three years when he worked at Merrill Lynch. He had volunteered to serve on a hastily assembled foreign policy council for the Trump campaign because of his time in Russia, his business interests, and the doctorate degree he held. Sam Clovis, who was overseeing the policy team at the beginning of the campaign, decided to invite Page to the one meeting. Page, however, never actually even attended the foreign policy meeting he was supposed to be part of. In testimony that he would later give to Congress, he would say that he "never spoke with [President Trump] in [his] life."

Carter Page was never authorized to speak in public on behalf of the Trump campaign. When Page, as a private citizen, was invited to give a commencement address in 2016 to the New Economic School in Moscow, the school where President Obama delivered a commencement speech in 2009, Corey explicitly informed him in an email that he could only do it on his own, and he did not represent or have any affiliation with the campaign. It was one of the only times Corey remembers actually communicating with Page. From what we now know, Page reportedly kept his word and didn't talk about the Trump campaign while he was in Russia.

The dossier, however, much to the joy of some senior members of the FBI, said otherwise. According to Christopher Steele—who heard the stories from sources who heard them from other sources who maybe heard them from other sources who were even less connected than he was—Carter Page had several illegal meetings with Russians. One of them, Steele writes, was a Russian businessman who offered him 19 percent stock in a Russian energy company, allegedly in exchange for easier sanctions on Russia if Trump got elected. Not only is this an enormous sum of money—Page would have made close to a billion dollars on the deal—but it would have been an outrageous one to offer someone who volunteered on a presidential campaign for a candidate who was never supposed to win the presidency.

Beyond the ridiculous fake energy cover story, the dossier also alleged that Page had "meetings" with many people who were working in the Russian government at the time of his visit. Most of these, we would later find, were just handshakes after his speech and brief conversations in lobbies and hallways. But the Democrats in Congress, particularly Adam Schiff (D-CA), would be all too happy to paint these quick encounters as hour-long meetings in which matters of national security and trade were discussed. During Schiff's opening statement at a congressional hearing, he went on for a few minutes about the deal, trying his best to insinuate not only that Carter Page was offered a deal in exchange for relief from sanctions, but that the Russian government had some kind of *kompromat* (the Russian term for compromising information used in blackmail) against Donald Trump and would use it if the traditional means of influence-peddling didn't work.

"According to Steele's Russian sources," Schiff said, "Page is offered brokerage fees by [Igor Sechin, the Russian businessman in question] on a deal involving a 19 percent share of the company. According to Reuters, the sale of a 19.5 percent share of [the company] later takes place with unknown purchasers and unknown brokerage fees. Is it a coincidence that the Russian gas company, Rosneft, sold a 19 percent share after former British intelligence officer

Steele was told by Russian sources that Carter Page was offered fees on a deal of just that size?"

We're not sure if you could follow that, but it's difficult for a reason. Democrats have a habit of making things much more complicated than they need to be so that people believe there's something when there's nothing. It's been the method behind the entire Russia investigation from the start. We actually do know why this Russian company sold off its shares after talking with Carter Page, and who bought them. None of the companies who bought these shares had anything to do with Page. If you're interested—we can't imagine you are—you can read all about it in the work of Elena Mazneva and Ilya Arkhipov, who covered the story for Russian media. But it seems that no one at the FBI reads international newspapers, because within days of getting a briefing on the dossier, Carter Page became the bureau's primary target for surveillance.

Peter Strzok seems to have singled him out personally, and he would later conduct a media leak strategy to smear his name in public. But first he needed to obtain a warrant to listen in on Page's—no relation to his mistress, by the way—communications.

It's worth noting that as soon as the FBI read the dossier and found what it believed (wrongly) to be damning information about Carter Page, the Crossfire Hurricane team could have brought him in for an interview to clear things up. This is standard operating procedure and falls into the category of "regular investigative methods" as defined by the FBI. In fact, the FISA application process explicitly states that a FISA warrant should not be sought until the intelligence agency in question has exhausted all other avenues of investigation. That means research, which the FBI hadn't done on Carter Page beyond one quick read of the dossier; extensive interviews, which it hadn't even attempted; and even in-person surveillance using an informant—something that the FBI had already tried and failed to do with Carter Page using Stefan Halper, their old spy buddy from Cambridge. The fact that none of these investigative avenues had yielded anything even close to incriminating information should have given the FBI the signal that it was time to stop and move on to something else. Any normal head of an FBI investigation—one who didn't have a deep hatred for the person he was investigating, perhaps, or one who didn't think he had a friendly FISA judge waiting to grant any application he put forward—would have done just that.

But Peter Strzok, according to his testimony and text messages, had become far too enraged for that. All throughout August and September, he fumed about Trump and started making plans to conduct surveillance on Trump. This would culminate in another FISA warrant on Carter Page in October, which, unlike their first attempt, would be accepted without reservation. But first he and the rest of the Crossfire Hurricane team had to make some show of trying to investigate Donald Trump the old-fashioned way, through in-person interviews and non-illegal methods of surveillance. It wouldn't yield much, but it was important to give the investigation validity, and to get to what they really wanted, which was a warrant to "tap the wires" in Trump Tower.

The first order of business was to send two agents to London, where George Papadopoulos had divulged his knowledge of Russian hacking operations to an Australian diplomat. Peter Strzok was one of them. This operation was kept so secret that only a small number of officials in the entire FBI knew about it, and it actually went against several norms of diplomacy, which allows for diplomats not to be interviewed by foreign intelligence agencies. Perhaps because of intimidation or due to the close personal friendship between President Obama and Prime Minister Malcolm Turnbull, the Australian government agreed to break this long-established norm and allowed Alexander Downer, the diplomat, to be interviewed.

We don't know what the Australian diplomat revealed, but we can assume it must have been about the rumors of Russian hacking that George Papadopoulos had divulged to him back in March. Now that the emails were out on the internet and being traced back to several sources, Papadopoulos looked as if he had known something in advance—maybe, they thought, he had even been a part of it. What began as a harmless piece of gossip that Papadopoulos never should have divulged was now something that could get him into trouble with the FBI. Over the next few months, Peter Strzok would use that as leverage against Papadopoulos.

A few days after he returned from London, Strzok got a text from his girlfriend, Lisa Page. They had been watching Trump's feud with the Khan family, who insulted Trump on television and prompted an angry Twitter response. Here is that exchange, which is as damning as anything the two love birds have ever said:

Page: This is not to take away from the unfairness of it all, but we are both deeply fortunate people . . . And maybe you're meant to stay where you are because you're meant to protect the country from that menace.

Strzok: Thanks. It's absolutely true that we're both very fortunate. And of course I'll try and approach it that way. I just know it will be tough at times. I can protect our country at many levels . . . not sure if that helps . . .

It's important to remember the context here. Strzok and Page were watching with disgust as Trump began his march to victory over Hillary Clinton, whom they both admired very much. (Other text messages show the two of them sharing glowing articles about Hillary Clinton and congratulating each other when good things happen to her.) At the time, Strzok was perhaps the one person in the country with the legal authority to make Trump's life very difficult. If he wanted to, he could have hauled everyone in the campaign in for an interview and held up our progress exponentially. He had already publicized the Russia hoax to such an extent that it was on nearly every news channel in the summer of 2016.

If we were looking back on their conversations up to August 8, 2016, reasonable people could disagree about whether Strzok actually had plans to stop Donald Trump from becoming president by using the full power of the FBI. The evidence was all circumstantial at the time.

But on August 8, late at night, he made a startling admission to Page, who was again worried about the prospect of Donald Trump becoming president. It's an admission so outlandish it proves beyond any doubt that the conspiracy to stop Trump went to the highest levels of the Justice Department and the FBI.

Page: He's not ever going to become president, right? Right?!

Strzok: No. No he's not. We'll stop it.

For about two months after this message was sent, Strzok and the rest of the Crossfire Hurricane team interviewed as many sources as they could find to try to link Paul Manafort, George Papadopoulos, Carter Page, and Michael Flynn to Russia. In the case of Manafort this was simple. He had been an international businessman most of his life, and it was only a matter of time before someone noticed. An inexperienced rookie investigator could have indicted him for conspiracy and fraud. On August 15, it was revealed that he'd taken about $12.7 million in cash payments from pro-Russia groups in Ukraine. There was much more where that came from. Five days later, on August 20, he was fired as campaign chairman, proving everyone who tried to keep him away from the Trump campaign in the first place absolutely correct. But as we've said before, things were a mess in the early days of the campaign. It's no surprise that a grifter like Manafort was able to dupe some people and weasel his way in—at least for a little while.

On Flynn, the case was also pretty easy. Thanks to meetings he'd been taking as the head of DIA—meetings like the one in Cambridge University covered in chapter 2—it wasn't difficult to give the impression that he had spoken to Russians or Russian agents. This is something that Stefan Halper, who was still doing his best to infiltrate the Trump campaign staff, knew very well, and something he would use against Flynn during the president-elect's transition. This, combined with a few mistakes on Flynn's part, would be his undoing. With George Papadopoulos, the case was open-and-shut. The FBI had interviewed the Australian diplomat he spoke with in London who said Papadopoulos told him that he "knew" about Russian hacking before any of it even happened. The Crossfire Hurricane team was in a position to nail three out of four targets right away.

The only one they couldn't pin down was Carter Page. All throughout August and September, it seemed to be clear to everyone on the team that the next step in the investigation would be to go back to the Foreign Intelligence Surveillance Court and get a warrant to spy on him. They would use the fake dossier as evidence, hiding its origins so that the judge would finally grant them permission. Strzok was personally involved in drafting the warrant, which he sent to Sally Yates and the Justice Department in the fall.

The text messages between Lisa Page and Strzok continued during this time. They were still having a steamy affair and trying to keep it secret from their spouses by using their government-issued devices for all communications. On August 15, they were in a meeting together in the office of Andrew McCabe, Jim Comey's deputy, who had played a significant role in clearing Hillary Clinton from all blame during the investigation of her emails. To this day, it has not been revealed exactly what was discussed in Andy's office, but this meeting is widely believed to be when senior members of the FBI agreed to put in place an "insurance policy" against Donald Trump. Here is what Page and Strzok texted afterward—it's alarming enough to nullify the entire Crossfire Hurricane investigation and send everyone involved to prison.

> Page: I want to believe the path you threw out for consideration in Andy's office—that there's no way he

gets elected—but I'm afraid we can't take that risk. It's like an insurance policy in the unlikely event you die before you're 40.

Less than a month later, on September 2, Lisa Page sent Strzok another text, this one about Barack Obama and his interest in the case against Donald Trump. "[The president] wants to know everything we're doing," she said. It seems that even Barack Obama, who at that time was actively campaigning for Hillary and against Trump, was getting worried about Trump's chances of winning and wanted to know what Strzok's "insurance policy" was all about. We don't know when Obama was informed about what the Crossfire Hurricane team was doing, but we do know that a little over a month after Lisa Page told Strzok that Obama needed to be informed about "everything [they were] doing," the FBI, with the full knowledge of Sally Yates, filed for a FISA warrant to spy on Carter Page.

CHAPTER 7

SURVEILLANCE ABUSE

WITH THE HELP AND KNOWLEDGE from the top echelons of the U.S. government, the Crossfire Hurricane team was just picking up steam, collecting information on several members of the Trump campaign, when a startling discovery was made in New York. There, in one of the FBI's Manhattan field offices, special agents came across a bombshell on the laptop of Anthony Weiner, the disgraced former Democrat congressman from New York.

Weiner, as you may remember, had a habit of texting lewd photographs of himself to women other than his wife. When it was revealed that one of those young women was actually very young—a fifteen-year-old girl living in South Carolina, to be exact—the FBI got involved and obtained a search warrant that would allow them to comb through all of Weiner's electronic devices for more evidence. The warrant limited their search to Weiner's two cell phones, one office computer, and a laptop that he shared with his family. According to the warrant, only the messages that had either been sent or received by Weiner pertaining to their sex crime investigation were fair game—everything else, no matter how serious, fell outside the scope of their investigation.

As the FBI initiated the search, on September 26, 2016, however, investigators found a startling discovery—something they couldn't ignore. Somewhere on the hard drive, nestled perhaps between racy texts and explicit photos of the congressman's private parts, agents happened upon something like 600,000 emails belonging to none other than former secretary of state Hillary Rodham Clinton.

It was actually Weiner's wife, Huma Abedin, who had sent and received most of the emails. Abedin had been with Hillary Clinton for nearly as long as she had been in public life, from a brief stint in the Clinton White House all the way through Hillary's campaigns for the Senate and the presidency. From 2009 to 2013, she worked in the State Department with Clinton. This meant that Abedin was looped in on nearly every email chain and query that crossed Clinton's inbox during that four-year period.

Often, Abedin would work from home, using the laptop that she shared with her husband to correspond with the secretary. This whole shared laptop situation alone, by the way, is actually quite a serious crime, given that the use of the laptop would have enabled Anthony Weiner to access some of our nation's most serious classified materials (and we all know how well he can keep a secret). Even if he had been a top government official, which he wasn't, viewing that kind of material without authorization would have had serious consequences.

On September 28, 2016, the head of the New York office of the FBI notified the top brass in Washington, D.C., which included forty senior FBI executives, including Deputy Director Andrew McCabe, about the new emails. None of them had any interest in reopening the Clinton email case. James Comey had already exonerated Hillary Clinton in July, and they felt that having the public find out that there were more emails all along would make them look very bad.

But the special agents in New York who had found the emails needed an answer. None of them had the proper clearance to review the emails themselves. They weren't even authorized to open the files. They had notified FBI leadership in the hope that someone would get a warrant to review all of the new emails—a warrant that would arrive only with the expressed authorization of James Comey. All McCabe had to do was let Comey know and have someone draft the warrant. But when the head of the New York field office alerted the FBI's deputy director, McCabe told . . . no one. The number two person at the FBI did not notify his superior, did not write a memo to the file, did not alert anyone at the Department of Justice or the inspector general—Andy McCabe did nothing.

For a while, the information about the new Clinton emails just lingered around the deputy director's office. Had McCabe lit a fire under investigators on September 28, when he first learned about the new emails, there might have been time to properly review them before the election. Instead he eventually assigned the case to a team in the FBI's Hoover Building that could keep it grinding through their administrative gears for another month, until after the election. One of those gear grinders was none other than Peter Strzok, the man who had so purposefully bungled the first investigation into Clinton's emails. Needless to say, Strzok applied the same stellar work ethic this time around.

"This isn't a ticking terrorist bomb," he said, trying to bring the bureau's attention to what he believed were more pressing matters—the Russia investigation.

For twenty-six days, McCabe, Strzok, and his team did nothing with the new emails. Sensing that there was something wrong, one of the New York agents who had originally come across the emails traveled to Washington to speak with Peter Strzok directly, forcing his hand and making him pick up the pace on his investigation into Clinton. The next day, along with the rest of the team that had conducted the original "investigation" into Hillary Clinton's emails—the one that had been code-named Midyear Exam—they briefed James Comey on what they had found. All they needed was a new search warrant and they would be free to start digging through the tens of thousands of new emails.

Everyone in the building knew that thanks to the lengthy process involved in obtaining a search warrant, any investigation that began on that day could never be completed by the election. Voters were going to cast their ballots in twelve days. But the Midyear Exam team met with Director Comey anyway, describing the new trove of emails to him and remarking that this batch was ten times larger than the one they had reviewed previously. They also noted that the new batch might contain the infamous "smoking gun" email, and that some of the messages covered the elusive two-month period during which Clinton is supposed to have set up the private email server in her home. All they needed was Comey's approval, they said, and they would be able to obtain a new search warrant and begin digging.

According to his own account of the situation, Comey gave his permission for the team to obtain a warrant "immediately." He must have known that the details of that meeting would someday become public, and that his response to the situation would be recorded and heavily scrutinized, because this is exactly what he should have done. His permission gave the green light to begin the investigation that the FBI should have done a year ago.

The man who received his orders, however, wasn't so forward-thinking. Because he had the most experience, it was Strzok's job to file the warrant that would allow him to search Hillary Clinton's new emails. Since he had known about the new emails for much longer than Comey—since roughly the end of September—he should have had a warrant ready to go. But he didn't.

As the head of the Crossfire Hurricane investigation, he had a different warrant on his mind—one that had already been approved.

On October 15, 2016, a DOJ line attorney returned to the courthouse with a cleaner FISA application than the one they had brought in June. Unlike the one that had been summarily rejected four months earlier, this one was much narrower in scope, and only sought a warrant to spy on one person: Carter Page. There was *no crime* listed on this application for the warrant, and nothing to insinuate—at least in any real sense—that Carter Page might eventually commit a crime. In 2014, Page actually helped the FBI to prosecute a case against Russian agents, using his expertise in the country to do so. He had been on the FBI's team in that case, fighting against Russia for the good of the United States. This makes the betrayal he suffered at the hands of Strzok and the Crossfire Hurricane team all the more unsettling.

From a purely legal standpoint, according to our sources, even if the FBI had good reason to believe that Page would be recruited by the Russians—which it didn't—this still wouldn't have been enough to get a FISA warrant on him. There is no crime in being a target of Russian spies, only of being one. It would be like the police asking to spy on someone because they think he might get robbed; it doesn't make any sense. But the FBI, having found out that Page was a volunteer on Donald Trump's foreign policy council, decided that he was their best shot at framing Trump. If they could listen in on his phone calls, they thought, some ancillary information might come their way that would make the candidate himself look bad. Again, at the door of the Foreign Intelligence Surveillance Court, Sally Yates' DOJ lawyers met their counterparts from the Department of Justice and other lawyers from the NSA. Peter Strzok and James Comey were not present, but their lawyers from the FBI were.

The new application was reportedly clean, and it contained lots of information that the lawyer from the NSA had provided, including things like emails and phone calls that the NSA had collected "incidentally" as part of its wireless wiretapping program—a program just like the one James Comey had edited himself after rushing to the bedside of Attorney General John Ashcroft with Bob Mueller. Other than this dubiously sourced material, however, the only other shred of evidence that the FBI and DOJ could provide was the fake Steele dossier, which was listed on the application as "research," free of any mention that the Democrat National Committee or Hillary Clinton had actually been the ones who paid for its creation. The reason that the fake Steele dossier had been needed in the first place, of course, was that the FBI had already spied on Carter Page once and found nothing. In order to get permission a second time, they would need extremely convincing new evidence. To do this, they needed to convince the FISA court not only that the dossier and its author, Christopher Steele, were more credible than they actually were, but that the claims could be substantiated in some other place. In investigations that would be conducted by the House Permanent Select Committee on Intelligence in the months following Donald Trump's election, investigators in Congress, led by Devin Nunes, would come to find that the FBI had been extremely reckless in coming up with this new evidence, even going so far as to leave out information and lie about its sources.

The House intel committee would find, for example, that Steele had repeatedly made his hatred of Donald Trump very clear to Bruce Ohr, the number four person at the Justice Department who played an enormous role in getting the dossier to the top of the government (if you'll remember, Bruce Ohr's wife, Nellie Ohr, had been one of the people involved in compiling the dossier in the first place). Steele had told Ohr that he was "desperate that Donald Trump not get elected and was passionate about him not being president." This bias was recorded repeatedly in the FBI files about Christopher Steele, but not included on the warrant to spy on Carter Page. The relationship between the Ohrs, Glenn Simpson, and Christopher Steele was also concealed from the FISA court. Perhaps most egregious of all, the House intel committee revealed that the only other source of information pertaining to Carter Page was an article in Yahoo News, which had been written by Michael Isikoff, who had a long-standing relationship with Glenn Simpson. What the FBI decided not to include on the application—even though the information was well-known to them at the time—was that the only source for that story had been none other than Christopher Steele, the man who wrote the phony dossier in the first place.

There was hardly a single piece of information on the warrant to spy on Carter Page that did not trace back in some way to Steele, the man who by that point had been discredited. It's a miracle he was allowed to keep his job. In footnote 8 of the FISA application, the lengths to which the FBI went to conceal its sources become very clear. Here it is, printed in full—see if you can figure out who's who:

> Source #1 was approached by an identified U.S. person, who indicated to Source #1 that a U.S.-based law firm had hired the identified U.S. person to conduct research regarding Candidate #1's ties to Russia. (The identified U.S. person and Source #1 have a long-standing business relationship.) The identified U.S. person hired Source #1 to conduct this research. The identified U.S. person never advised Source #1 as to the motivation behind the research into Candidate #1's ties to Russia. The FBI speculates that the identified U.S. person was likely looking for information that could be used to discredit Candidate #1's campaign.

Still with us? This footnote was printed in such small

type among so many other unclear footnotes that it's unknown if the FISA judge even read it. The footnote does not name Hillary Clinton or the DNC at all. This is strange, considering that the dossier had been paid for almost entirely by these two entities. It is only mentioned that the entity that paid for the fake dossier was a "law firm." As we're sure you've noticed, there are hundreds of thousands of law firms in the United States, many of which could have paid for this fake dossier. Saying that it was a U.S. law firm that paid to compile the fake dossier was an obvious attempt by the FBI to conceal the origins of the document so that the Crossfire Hurricane team could get permission to spy on Carter Page. They knew that at the time, only 2 percent of FISA applications were rejected, and only for blatantly violating the law—just as they had been told back in June, when their first shot at a FISA warrant was rejected.

Somehow, with the NSA information and the fake dossier on its side, the FBI and DOJ were granted their FISA warrant, which gave them permission to tap the phones of Page and, by extension, a few other members of the Trump campaign. Although Page had stopped volunteering for the campaign at this time, the FBI continued to surveil him counting on him still being in contact with people on the campaign. This was the same "incidental intelligence" they had been denied for in June, but doing it more cleverly this time. Perhaps because of how easy this had been to get away with, the FBI soon broadened the scope of its investigation to include Roger Stone and Michael Flynn as well. By the beginning of November, the Crossfire Hurricane team was listening in on Carter Page.

Peter Strzok, who was leading the charge and listening

for any chance to take down Trump, seemed to grow more repulsed by the Republican nominee every day. Five days after he obtained the FISA warrant to spy on members of the Trump campaign, he texted girlfriend and FBI attorney Lisa Page about a debate he was watching. Here is part of the exchange:

> Strzok: I am riled up. Trump is a fucking idiot, is unable to provide a coherent answer . . . I CAN'T PULL AWAY. WHAT THE FUCK HAPPENED TO OUR COUNTRY??!?!

The rest of that message, which may have contained sensitive information, is, at this writing, still redacted. But that doesn't really matter. What matters is that we now know exactly what was going through Strzok's head as he built his case against the Trump campaign. He wasn't doing it because he believed there was actually a crime or a case to be made against them. In fact, not long after he returned from London to interview the diplomat with whom Papadopoulos spoke, he wrote: "I cannot believe we are seriously looking at these allegations and the pervasive connections." Rather, he was doing it because he and the rest of the Crossfire Hurricane team were grasping for absolutely anything that might incriminate Donald Trump—even things they knew to be false and based on lies.

While he was looking for an angle on Trump, Strzok made a show of filing a warrant to search Hillary's emails on October 30—only eight days before the election, when he knew there wouldn't be time to fully execute on it. He made heavy edits to the warrant on his home computer, which is another breach of FBI protocol. Then he took a break from Crossfire Hurricane and apparently pretended to go through a bunch of Clinton's emails.

In the days following the election, James Comey would give a heroic account of what his team was able to do. According to testimony he gave in front of Congress, specialized agents had performed what he calls "technological wizardry," separating the emails they had from ones they had already seen and scanning them in seconds for key words. He said that the team had spent weeks going through them before he made the decision to exonerate Clinton of all blame a second time.

Not surprisingly, almost nothing Comey said during that testimony turned out to be true. The actual investigation lasted only a day and was controlled completely by Strzok and two other agents whose names we still don't know. During the "investigation," Strzok kept up a lively correspondence with his mistress, Lisa Page. They talked about how worried they were about Donald Trump becoming president, and how often it seemed like they, the FBI, would be powerless to stop him from winning the election. While Strzok was in the midst of deciding what to do about Hillary's emails—something that surely would have affected the outcome of the election if it had been conducted properly—Strzok texted Page the following message:

Strzok: We're going to make sure the right thing is done. Don't worry.

Sure enough, just a few days after Strzok sent the message to his girlfriend, the FBI's lawyers announced that by using their "technical wizardry," they had managed to condense the original package of 694,000 emails down to just 6,827. They gave no details as to how they had managed such an unlikely feat, saying only that many of the emails were duplicates or personal in nature. Then another lawyer at the FBI cut the number down to just 3,077, saying she had excluded all emails that were either personal in nature or fell outside the scope of the investigation. She also gave no sign of how she had made these decisions. The remaining emails were then divided into three groups of about one thousand emails each, which Peter Strzok and two other agents managed to review in just under twelve hours.

On November 6, Director Comey sent an official letter to Congress, saying that despite the new information and the massive number of new emails the FBI hadn't been able to review, their opinion on the matter "hadn't changed." In the judgment of Comey on behalf of the FBI, Hillary Clinton still should not be prosecuted for her crimes. Though still furious at Comey for humiliating their candidate on national TV, Hillary supporters breathed a sigh of relief in the hope that the email "matter" was behind them. Hillary Clinton, they believed, would be able to assume the office of the President of the United States without any baggage and free of scandal. All they cared about now was embarrassing Trump.

This is an attitude that pervaded the FBI from the start of the investigation all the way through election night. The objective was never to uncover any real crimes; it was only to hurt the public image of Donald Trump. No one on the FBI's Crossfire Hurricane team was sure whether there was anything to be found, but they pressed ahead anyway. Throughout October, the public seemed to be only half-supportive of the FBI's efforts. Even the *New York*

Times, which was usually against whatever Trump was for, had published a story before the election wondering whether the investigation was worth doing at all. The headline read: "Investigating Donald Trump, the FBI Sees No Clear Link to Russia."

The body of the story, which is shocking to read today, considering the virtual 180-degree spin the *Times* has taken, contains a few salient observations, some of which are reprinted here:

> For much of the summer, the FBI pursued a widening investigation into a Russian role in the American presidential campaign. Agents scrutinized advisers close to Donald J. Trump, looked for financial connections with Russian financial figures, searched for those involved in hacking the computers of the Democrats, and even chased a lead—which they ultimately came to doubt—about a possible secret channel of email communication from the Trump Organization to a Russian bank.

If you'll notice, the "lead" that the newspaper refers to is the one the FBI tried to get a FISA warrant for—the one that was thrown out of court by a judge who caught on to their illegal spy games early. If the system were operating properly, that would have been the end of the Russia investigation for good. The article also made some mention of the hacked emails from the Democrat National Committee that George Papadopoulos was in trouble for talking about, saying that "even the hacking of the [DNC emails], the FBI and intelligence officials now believe, was aimed at disrupting the presidential election rather than electing Mr. Trump." In the end, the *Times* said, correctly, that "none of the investigations so far have found any conclusive or direct link between Mr. Trump and the Russian government."

For a while, that was exactly what most people thought. They rightly saw that the fake Russian collusion narrative was only an excuse cooked up by the Never-Trump Republicans and the Democrats to explain how someone had so radically beat their system and risen to the top without the usual combination of establishment support and lavish donations.

That all changed on election night. Suddenly what had once been an investigation into a long-shot candidate— one that they believed would go away as soon as the FBI's favored candidate, Hillary Clinton, won the election— became an urgent plot to take down a duly elected president. Suddenly Comey was scrambling, trying to cover his tracks on the Hillary email investigation and looking for ways to go after Trump without seeming biased. Peter Strzok was doubling his efforts to go after Trump, who was now the president-elect.

These efforts culminated in what we've called "the handoff," when Comey went to Trump Tower and slipped the dossier into a meeting with the president-elect, knowing that as soon as he did it, the media would have no choice but to run with the story. It was the first shot in the Deep State's war against Trump, and it was fired to nullify the election and bring down the president before he was even inaugurated.

CHAPTER 8

THE MORNING AFTER

WHEN COREY FIRST JOINED the Trump team in January 2015, he was given a small office on the twenty-fourth floor of Trump Tower. From there Corey worked every day for hours, trying to come up with a way to convince Mr. Trump to announce he was running for president. With his many years of experience on campaigns, Corey thought he would be able to run a campaign that could help Trump win in New Hampshire and beyond. What Corey learned very quickly and what many others still haven't figured out was how to Let Trump Be Trump—that wasn't just a few words, it was a mantra.

Corey found out very quickly how the twenty-sixth floor of Trump Tower worked. That included how Donald J. Trump made decisions. Corey knew not to encumber Trump with PowerPoint presentations that were developed by people who attended Harvard Business School. Mr. Trump was always learning. Whether he was conducting a radio interview or listening to some TV pundits, he was absorbing information. Mr. Trump did not want to be inundated with process; he was a disrupter while also being an innovator. Process was the problem, not the solution. Donald Trump ran his business by gut feeling, listening to all sides of an issue, then making a decision and executing. Often Mr. Trump would empower whoever brought him a new idea to execute it regardless of their role in the organization. He would say something like, "I like it, go get it done."

You see, Donald Trump is an active listener and knows a good idea when he hears one. During meetings, he's inquisitive and continually poses questions to challenge basic assumptions that are the status quo. When the election was over, we would see once again a new team attempting to process Donald Trump to death because that's the way they have always done it and that's why they would ultimately fail. If the leadership team would have embraced Mr. Trump's innate management style, which was extremely successful, the White House would have been a very different place—a place that would have been filled with people who wanted to support the America First agenda instead of liberals and elitists.

On the morning of November 9, 2016, at around nine o'clock, as one of his first official acts as a "transition official," Dave walked into Steve Bannon's office and sat down on one of the old, tattered chairs we had used for furniture on the campaign. He flipped through a thick file on foreign policy while Bannon finished up a phone conversation—not a pleasant one, from the sound of it.

As the voice on the other end of the line grew fainter and more nervous, Dave couldn't help but listen closely to Steve's end of the conversation. Sometimes that could be fun.

"Well, we kind of need you here, like, now," he said. "You're in charge of presidential appointments for the transition."

There was a long pause on the other end of the line, the kind that comes before bad news.

" . . . flights?" Steve said. "Why are you looking at flights? I thought you were in Manhattan. Where did you—"

At this point, Dave realized Bannon was on the phone with Bill Haggerty, an equities trader who was the Tennessee finance chairman for a Trump SuperPAC, and whom we had put in charge of presidential appointments in 2016. He was one of about fourteen members of the presidential transition team, which had just become one of the most important groups of people in the world. It was their job to staff the government, conduct cabinet interviews, and prepare legislation for President-elect Trump's first months in office.

Steve had been looking through some of the team's notes all morning, and very few of them made any sense. His first order of business had been to get Haggerty into the building right away.

Watching Steve's face go from its usual sunset red to very pale, it became clear that something was wrong with Haggerty. When Bannon hung up the phone, Dave could sense that the team was in trouble—he only hoped that the head of the transition was all right.

"He's in the Bahamas," Bannon said.

"You're joking," Dave said.

"Nope. He said he'd be back in a few days."

Haggerty must have been reading the *New York Times*. As you might remember, the newspaper had given Trump only a 2–3 percent chance of victory, mostly so their readers could feel like they were watching a real fight. Haggerty had decided to take a vacation for about two weeks, starting just before election night. He probably figured that the inevitable Hillary victory would be easier to endure while he was having a margarita or two on the beach. So, when the boss won, and it came time for him to get started, he was a few thousand miles away, and probably a little behind on the appointments process, to say the least.

Dave looked at Bannon and laughed. Sometimes that's all you can do. For the most part, he stayed calm behind the desk. Throughout the campaign, even during the darkest days after the Billy Bush tape surfaced, Steve was Mr. Steady. He never wavered in his faith that Donald Trump would beat Hillary Clinton. When people asked him Trump's chances of winning, he would reply, "One hundred percent. No question." It became his favorite phrase. Steve would later go on to make some stupid mistakes, say some stupid things, but he never lost his complete belief in the president.

Now, after the first big blow of the transition process—which had occurred, in a sign of things to come, before breakfast on the first day—Steve displayed similar resolve. He sighed, and then gestured at the folder in front of him. Dave laughed again, but a bit more despairingly this time.

During his first day on the job as deputy campaign manager, back in August 2016, Dave had looked through the drawers in his desk. Along with a couple of ketchup packets and loose rubber bands, there was a high-gloss paperback-sized book with *The Romney Readiness Project* printed on the cover page. Complete with flowcharts and graphs, it was a comprehensive playbook on how to organize a government. Romney had named every appointment and every secretary—from agriculture down to the typists and stenographers in the West Wing. He'd even decided where most of the offices would be. With that kind of guidance, we might have had a leg up on things, except for the fact that the Romney Readiness Project, or anything else associated with the transition, was never discussed with candidate Trump.

As you may or may not know, Donald Trump is a superstitious man. He's the type of guy who'll throw salt over his shoulder, steer clear of ladders, and never, ever plan for things that haven't happened yet. He thinks that acting like you've already won—or even entertaining the thought that you might win—screws with your chances of actually winning. Throughout the campaign, he called this "bad juju." He told us "not to jinx it."

Every time either of us felt like laughing at that, we'd remember that it worked. Mitt Romney, on the other hand, who took a week off from his campaign in September 2012 to focus on the details of his transition, ended up losing the race in a landslide. The same goes for Hillary Clinton, who by November 2016 was already picking out carpets and drapes for the Oval Office. She was taking time off from the campaign to get a good rest before the big move to D.C. As we've said before, you can't argue with success.

On the other hand, the president-elect's superstitions left us without a coherent strategy to fill the 4,152 presidential appointee positions that he has in the federal government, including about four hundred positions directly on the White House campus. Some of these positions would eventually be filled by people who never supported Donald Trump's agenda or likely even voted for him. Once enough of these swamp creatures got in, they were all but impossible to get out.

Bannon had read the Romney book about three times. Knowing what the appointments are is one thing; knowing whom to appoint is something completely different. Our pool of candidates, which we had sworn early on would include absolutely zero liberals or Never-Trump Republicans, was minuscule compared to most incoming administrations. But the names were familiar, which was a good thing.

That morning, we knew that Jared Kushner and Kellyanne Conway would come aboard in key roles. Stephen Miller would be a senior advisor and speechwriter, and Steve Mnuchin wanted to be secretary of the Treasury. We knew that Hope Hicks would have an important function in President Trump's orbit, and that Dan Scavino would probably continue handling social media. Beyond that, there were few roles that we knew for certain were going to be filled by Trump supporters. Sure, Keith Schiller, John McEntee, and George Gigicos would be given the opportunity to move to Washington, D.C., to be part of the team, but, shy of a few others, everything else was up in the air.

There was much discussion about General Mike Flynn joining as the national security advisor—he had been a supporter of Donald Trump from the time Mr. Trump won the Nevada primary back in early 2016. He had also become famous (perhaps a little too famous) for leading a "lock her up" chant at the Republican National Convention in 2016. But before that, he had been one of the most respected figures in the U.S. Army—a man whose tenacious commitment to on-the-ground intelligence had gone a long way in turning the tide against the insurgency in Iraq and Afghanistan. He was committed to destroying ISIS in Iraq and Syria, just as Mr. Trump wanted. We knew too that when the Deep State came for Donald Trump—which it inevitably would—we needed someone smart on our side who knew his way around the intelligence community. For that, Michael Flynn seemed like our guy.

We never counted on the Deep State coming for *him* first.

After one last flip through its pages, Bannon held *The Romney Readiness Project* over the wastebasket in his office and winced. He opened his hand, and the manual hit the bottom of the basket with a thud.

"Haggerty isn't our only problem," he said.

The next day, Donald J. Trump traveled to the White House with his wife, Melania, son-in-law Jared Kushner, and Hope Hicks. Mr. Trump had come to Washington at the behest of President Obama.

None of us in Trump Tower that morning was quite sure how the meeting was going to go. After all, Donald Trump and Barack Obama hadn't exactly been kind to each other in the past. But President Obama had called on the night of the election and graciously offered to have the meeting. In keeping with tradition, Melania Trump would have tea with Michelle Obama, while Jared would go to meetings with members of Obama's senior staff, learning how to put the White House staff together. Even with the cooperation and planning, however, we'd be lying if we told you we weren't expecting some kind of fireworks.

When the president-elect and Mrs. Trump pulled up in the Beast (actually, it was a scaled-down version of the Beast, the president's limo, that was sent to pick them up), the Obamas were waiting at the South Lawn entrance of the White House to receive them. The two couples exchanged gifts and posed for pictures, then split off into pairs and stepped into the building. Photographers and reporters yelled questions from the road, but none of them were answered. Judging by what Corey had seen in CNN's Washington newsroom on election night, the reporters were probably still getting their blood pressure down from the election results.

After going inside, President Obama and President-elect Trump sat talking for a long time in the Oval Office, stretching what was supposed to have been a ninety-minute meeting into a freewheeling session that went well beyond three hours. You might have seen pictures of that day— all smiles, backslapping, and friendly handshakes. By all accounts, President-elect Trump truly enjoyed his meeting with President Obama that afternoon. Those smiles were all genuine, at least on Trump's part.

On the way back to Trump Tower from LaGuardia Airport, the president-elect called Corey from the secure phone in the car. Corey took the call in Dave's office. Mr. Trump was elated. It might have been the first time he ever spoke to Obama face-to-face. They talked about the Yankees and the Cubs and ESPN. "He's a regular guy!" the president-elect exclaimed.

Melania, too, had enjoyed the visit, having tea with Michelle Obama in the White House residence. The two then sat for an extended time on the Truman Balcony discussing their backgrounds and their children.

There was one thing about the meeting, however, that seemed odd to Mr. Trump.

President Obama had given Trump one unique piece of advice—something he hadn't asked for and wasn't quite sure what to do with now that he had it. Not that Mr. Trump minded. He was about to enter the most challenging job in the world, and Obama had been the president for eight years. He knew from staff briefings that it was customary for the current president to pass down advice and counsel to his successor. Obama offered this counsel—"North Korea is your single biggest national security threat," and second, he said, "Don't let anyone influence you on who to hire or not."

In light of these facts, the advice Obama had given Trump took us by surprise. Obama had prefaced the advice—more of a stern suggestion, really—by telling the boss that he should go with his gut when making decisions about his staff. "Don't listen to anyone who tries to talk you out of hiring who you want," the president had said, according to Trump. He followed up that statement, however, with an odd turn. Something much more specific. No more than a few minutes after providing that advice, Barack Obama told Donald Trump not to hire General Michael T. Flynn, one of the few people we were already seriously considering for a position in the administration. When President-elect Trump told us what Obama said later that day, it didn't come as much of a surprise. Only in looking back can we see how odd the suggestion was, especially considering what Obama had known about Flynn.

President-elect Trump was not only fond of Mike Flynn; he deeply respected his service to the country. There were good reasons for that respect. Flynn grew up in Rhode

Island as one of nine kids in a hardworking, blue-collar family. He loved sports, could surf, and had a good sense of humor. As a military intelligence commander, he was unsurpassed, and his contribution went a long way in finally turning the tide against the insurgencies in Iraq and Afghanistan. He flew up the ranks to lieutenant general. But on the way, he had also pissed many people off—including the forty-fourth President of the United States.

Flynn didn't like the status quo, he cared not a whit for the bureaucracy of the agencies he worked for, and thought Obama's White House was hamstringing military operations on the ground. For years Flynn had watched as the war against radical Islamic terrorism shifted from the battlefield, where he knew it belonged, to the dank basement offices of the White House. People say Obama aides like Susan Rice and Ben Rhodes had begun tacking wanted posters up on their walls, planning drone strikes on their own. The hunt for terrorist cells and anti-American insurgents had become little more than a video game to them. It was something they could do in the afternoon right after their Cobb salad lunch and never have to get their hands dirty. Meanwhile, their boss was on television pulling troops out of combat zones and falsely proclaiming that the war on terror was over. Flynn, unlike anyone in the Obama White House, had seen this war firsthand. He knew it was far from over. This, combined with the fact that he was also no fan of Hillary Clinton (as you might remember from the Trump rallies), made him a strong candidate to be Donald Trump's national security advisor.

Now, it wasn't as if Mike was perfect. Far from it; his disorganization during the transition used to drive Bannon crazy. "This could be a shit show," Steve would say. In

Michael Hastings' book *The Operators*, the book based on the *Rolling Stone* story that got Flynn's boss in Afghanistan, General Stanley McChrystal, fired, one of Flynn's staffers called him "a rat on acid." The same brain that made him a brilliant intelligence officer also made him one of the most disorganized. It was almost as though he had a genius strain of ADHD. But if it was the general's disorganization that prompted Obama's suggestion, he didn't tell that to the president-elect; at least the boss didn't tell us he did.

As President-elect Trump recalled his meeting with Obama that afternoon, we were tempted to think that Obama's aversion to Flynn was little more than a small annoyance—something he never should have said aloud but that had no real consequence in the end. We even toyed with the notion that Obama had simply been trying to get into Trump's head, thinking he could put our administration on its heels early out of spite. Knowing what we know today, that might have been the case. But it also could have been something much more sinister.

We have little doubt that Obama had let his intelligence agencies spiral out of control during his eight years in office, even going so far as to either implicitly or explicitly allow them to conduct surveillance on citizens of the United States on domestic soil—and not just any citizens, but members of the Trump campaign. The people at the top of his government were more left-leaning than in any administration in history, and they obviously felt threatened by the incoming Trump administration. For Obama's intelligence community, spy games like this were the rule rather than the exception.

Now that Flynn was slated to come in and take over as head of the National Security Council, he would have access to the most sensitive intelligence in the country. It's not unreasonable to assume that Obama knew Flynn could expose some of the misconduct in which his intelligence agencies had engaged—particularly when it came to the abuse of surveillance practices. He certainly knew that Flynn could do some damage to the permanent power structures of his intelligence agencies and shake up the bureaucracy he had helped to grow. Obama probably figured that if he could convince Trump in a private meeting—the details of which were never supposed to leak—not to hire Flynn in the first place, the chances of his illegal spying on American citizens ever coming to light would decrease dramatically.

President Obama, likely at the behest of the Deep State's leaders, such as then-CIA chief John Brennan, and the director of national intelligence (DNI), James Clapper, was going to do everything he could not to give Flynn a chance.

Though Obama's advice bothered the president-elect, it didn't diminish Mr. Trump's mood after meeting him. In the days ahead, Trump would frequently quote some of the things Obama had told him during their meeting in the White House, speaking as if the advice had come from an old friend. Despite their history as bitter rivals, President-elect Trump was ready to take over the White House with a collaborative spirit, retaining as many nonpartisan staffers as he could and cutting back on the insults to liberals on Twitter. By that point it had started to feel like punching down anyway. There was no fun in it anymore.

CHAPTER 9

INSIDE JOB

DURING THOSE EARLY DAYS in the transition, Dave Bossie would stand by the window in his office on the fourteenth floor of Trump Tower and look down onto Fifth Avenue. A three-block stretch of the famous boulevard was closed, blocked off with big concrete barricades to prevent a car bomb from exploding in front of the building. New York City ten-wheel dump trucks, parked bumper to bumper, formed a barricade around the building. The massive protests had already begun and the media circus had pulled into town.

Donald J. Trump had pulled off the greatest American political victory since the American Revolution. Newspapers from across the country that just before election day had given Trump a one percent chance of winning the election had finished delivering the sad news (at least to them) of his victory to the world. Their journalists had typed through tears, scrambling to include the elegant, inclusive

language of the president-elect's victory speech in the late
editions of their stories. It would be the last time many
of them reported what Donald Trump said with anything
resembling accuracy or fairness. During the Trump campaign and election, the media had gone from the investigative watchdog that gave you Watergate and the Pentagon
Papers to the communications department for the Deep
State, the Clinton-controlled Democrat Party, and establishment Washington—and that includes Bob Woodward
himself.

The press and the Washington bureaucrats—the
unelected former power brokers, composing the State
Department, Department of Justice, CIA, FBI, and countless other agencies under the purview of the executive
branch—were still in a fog, holding on to the hope that it
had all been a dream. The same was true of the establishment and Never-Trump Republicans, who'd staked their
careers on the certainty of a Trump loss.

None of them stayed in a fog for long, however.

It's not like we didn't know they would be coming for us.
When you run an outsider's campaign, you're going to have
an outsider's problems, too. You can't piss off the establishment every day for a couple of years and then expect
them to become your best friends when it's all over. We
knew things would be rough. Cooperation with Democrats
in Congress would probably be impossible, and many of
the supposedly "bipartisan" government officials from the
Obama administration wouldn't be working for us or with
us. We hoped that the Trump administration would end up
looking very much like our campaign—consisting only of
true believers, who were loyal to their president and sup-
portive of Donald Trump's America First agenda.

What we didn't know, however, was how many of Trump's enemies had already infiltrated our ranks or were planning to do so by the morning after the election. We didn't know that people in America's intelligence agencies had worked throughout the campaign to do opposition research on Donald Trump—then used that research to spy on him illegally—or that many prominent Beltway lawyers had helped them do it. We certainly couldn't have foreseen the lengths to which people at the very bottom of our government would go to stop Trump's agenda from becoming law, or how powerful the "administrative state" had become under Presidents Clinton, Bush, and Obama.

There were pointed attacks on the Trump campaign from the very beginning—some of which came from within the United States government, and others from without—and they came swiftly, before we could even react. Some of the repercussions still haunt the Trump White House today. While they might seem preventable looking back, it's become clear in the writing of this book that we never really had much of a chance.

Trump's enemies struck early, long before the boss ever set foot in the White House. They hit him hard, and they hit him at home, right on the good old fourteenth floor of Trump Tower.

In those early weeks of the presidential transition, the people coming out of the elevators at Trump Tower grew less and less recognizable. Some of them who paraded by were outright swamp creatures—sleazy lawyers and political hacks who had never met or supported Trump.

We called this alarming number of new visitors "the November Ninth Club" because they seemed to have turned magically into Trump supporters after the networks called the race. Some were even "Never-Trumpers," a phrase that had arisen during the campaign for Republicans and conservatives who had taken a so-called brave stand against Donald Trump. The name actually had come from inside-the-Beltway writers and "strategists" like George Will and Tim Miller, who, along with dozens of others of their ilk, pledged they would vote for anyone at all—even a liberal Democrat or a socialist, even Hillary Clinton—before giving their support to the rightful nominee of their party. Yet, like the rest of the November Ninth Club, after Mr. Trump won the election, many of them publicly changed their tunes—and some showed up at Trump Tower during the transition looking for a job.

As an example, let us introduce you to Joe Hagin. Hagin is the very definition of establishment Republican; in fact his career in Washington reaches all the way back to Ronald Reagan. He served both Presidents Bush and was George W. Bush's deputy chief of staff for all eight years of his term. He ran in a circle of people who were no friends of the president-elect, people who had been writing magazine pieces and takedowns about Donald Trump during the campaign. Yet there he was in Trump Tower interviewing for the same job he had under Bush 43.

The decision to hire Hagin as deputy chief of staff would come back to haunt the administration big-time. Because he knew how the White House functioned—the deputy chief in charge of operations is basically in charge of the White House complex—he knew how best to exploit the system, which he did.

Hagin would limit people's access to the building, deciding who could or couldn't see the president and how long it would take for someone to apply for a job in the White House. In addition to those responsibilities, he was in charge of the professional staff that oversaw security clearances and was briefed on at least three occasions about the security concerns in alleged abuser Rob Porter's background check, but he did nothing to prevent him from continuing to review classified information and serve next to the president. This, as we all know, led to weeks of bad press for the administration and would have been totally avoidable if Joe and other senior officials had done their jobs properly when they found out about the alleged domestic abuse by Porter.

Hagin was also directly responsible for bringing in Bill Hughes. An avowed Never-Trumper, Hughes published a message on Facebook that lambasted people who had the nerve to work for both George W. Bush and President Trump, as if one were somehow better than the other.

In part, the post read, "Some Bush 43 advance people do advance and other promotion for Trump. That simply astounds me. I cannot reconcile the two, unless the respect and admiration they professed to have for the Boss [Bush] years ago, and perhaps continue to profess today, was and is hollow and meaningless." The image of Trump's face was superimposed on Thomas the Train to indicate, we guess, that the Trump administration was going off the tracks. "I expect a stain on the careers and perhaps even lives that they cannot wash away," Hughes writes about the advance people. "That's sad, because I remember them as mostly moral, decent people."

Bill Hughes, by the way, is still employed in the White House.

* * *

Maybe the most prominent member of the November Ninth Club came to Trump Tower almost immediately following the election.

Dave first saw him when he walked out of his office that morning to grab a cup of coffee in the kitchen on the fourteenth floor. Sitting behind one of the intern desks out front was a large, bald man reading the *New York Times* (that should have been a dead giveaway). During the campaign, those intern desks had a somewhat transient nature, so Dave at first didn't give the man all that much thought. When the man was still sitting there after Dave had a few meetings and some time had passed, he decided to find out just who he was.

"I'm Dave Bossie," he said, introducing himself. "Can I help you?"

"No, no," the bald man said. "I'm Gary Cohn. I'm here to help out with some of the economic stuff."

Dave knew of Gary Cohn, of course. You don't hang around Steve Bannon as long as Dave has and not know Wall Street leadership by heart. Bannon had an investment banking firm and worked for Goldman Sachs. But Dave also knew Cohn by his political reputation.

Cohn is a liberal Democrat, and while he was president of Goldman Sachs, they gave Hillary Clinton nearly three-quarters of a million dollars to give a series of talks. Talks, not even speeches. Goldman Sachs itself was extremely anti-Trump. During the campaign they donated a measly five grand to the Trump campaign, while funneling hundreds of thousands to Hillary.

Self-important and very, very rich, Cohn is the quintessential "limousine liberal." In fact, he would try to convince the boss to appoint him secretary of the Treasury. Instead the president-elect went with Steven Mnuchin, a loyal supporter. There will be more about Cohn ahead, but for now please know he's the poster boy for the disloyal staff conspiring against President Trump, and he was looking for a job with the administration on day one, being appointed chair of the National Economic Council, a mere stepping-stone to his ultimate goal, the chairmanship of the Federal Reserve.

One of the reasons why enemies of Trump were able to crawl through the cracks those first days was that we weren't prepared. As we described in *Let Trump Be Trump*, candidate Trump wouldn't allow us to even talk to him about the transition during the campaign. He thought it would be bad luck. Still, we had to be prepared.

In April 2016, when it was almost certain that Mr. Trump was going to become the Republican nominee for president, the Center for Presidential Transition contacted the campaign asking for someone to attend a meeting to begin to set up a presidential transition team. Corey sent Michael Glassner, his deputy campaign manager. When Michael returned he reported the need to start preparing to take over the government should we win.

Accordingly, Corey could think of only one person who could serve as the head of the presidential transition team—a man who was a friend of the candidate, and who had overseen a large staff as a governor—Chris Christie. As the former head of the Republican Governors Association (RGA), he also knew Washington, D.C. Corey advocated for and ultimately helped to appoint Christie chairman of the Trump transition team in April 2016.

Governor Christie put together a small team and set up

an office in Washington, D.C., to begin the preparations necessary—they worked on a shoestring budget. Most of the staff didn't get paid and the work was largely thankless. It was the equivalent of building out a full government.

Before we go on to tell you more, you need to know that we like and respect Governor Christie. He is certainly not an enemy of Trump. His herculean efforts as chairman of the RGA raised over $100 million and helped pick up governorships for the party. During the campaign, we also learned he was stand-up, solid, a straight shooter. The two-time New Jersey governor is smart as all hell, and his endorsement of Mr. Trump during the presidential campaign was critical. It came at a time when Trump was still in the fight for his life.

Chris is the type of guy who, once he makes a commitment to something, stays with it. After he suspended his own bid for president and endorsed the boss, Christie stayed with Trump through thick and thin. We spent countless hours together on the campaign trail with Governor Christie. But the relationship between Chris Christie and Donald Trump is as complicated as it is long-standing.

One day, right after Governor Christie was hired, Steve Bannon went up to the residence to talk to Mr. Trump. When he walked in, the boss was yelling at Christie, who was sitting on the couch. On the table in front of Mr. Trump was the *Washington Post*, open to a story about his transition team holding a fund-raiser and raising four or five million dollars. The boss didn't know about the fund-raiser; hell, he barely even knew we had a real, operating transition team.

"Remember Romney?" he yelled. "He's walking around in his khakis with his transition team and what the hell did it get him? I'll tell you what. He lost!"

The governor tried to explain to Mr. Trump that it was a federal statute, and that according to projections, they had to raise about $12 million to pay for transition costs. As a matter of fact, Mitt Romney put a million and a half of his own money in during the late stages of his campaign to pay for transition staffers who, along with the volunteers, numbered a whopping five hundred.

Mr. Trump didn't want people who could contribute to his campaign giving money to the transition team. The reality was they were two legally different entities and giving to one did not preclude you from giving to the other. Moreover, one was a nonprofit and the other was set up with the explicit purpose of getting Donald J. Trump elected president of the United States.

Governor Christie chaired the transition team all the way up until Mr. Trump became President-elect Trump.

The reason Christie was let go from the Trump transition, however, had more to do with internal politics than any money he raised for the team.

With Governor Christie's departure, our transition team went through a transition of its own. Headed by Vice President–elect Mike Pence, it was staffed mostly with key members of the Trump family, some Capitol Hill staffers, and an influx from the swamp. This change put us back to square one. All the work Governor Christie and his team had done over the past seven months was quite literally thrown in the trash.

No one in Trump Tower had much experience—if any—with building a government from scratch, and it got even harder when anyone Donald Trump had ever met now came in clamoring for a job.

It's important to note that there was a big difference
between the transition and the campaign. While everything was just as chaotic on the campaign, everyone had
only one mission in mind, and that was to get Donald
Trump elected. On the transition, however, many of the
people in the building were self-motivated, swamp-based
creatures who didn't support Mr. Trump but were looking
for a way into the White House to subvert his agenda. They
were driven only by a need to get close to the president-elect
and assume the power that position allows. There was no
centralized goal driving everyone to succeed anymore,
at least with most of the people surrounding us. We, the
die-hards who had been on the team from the beginning,
were clawing our way back, trying to put the right team
in place. There were times on the campaign when we felt
overwhelmed. On the transition, however, we were overwhelmed and infiltrated by enemies.

One of the first positions that needed to be filled was
chief of staff, which, aside from the president and vice
president, is the most critical role in the West Wing. All
other transitional decisions would flow from that one. We
had watched as Bannon and Reince Priebus became, effectively, the only two viable options for the job. Ultimately,
of course, it was the president-elect's decision. His executive decision-making style is one where he gathers as much
information and asks as many people as he can for their
input. But Donald Trump was in territory where he was
wholly unfamiliar. In making the decision for his chief,
he ended up partly listening to Speaker of the House Paul
Ryan and Senate Majority Leader Mitch McConnell, who
told the president-elect that he needed a chief of staff who

was familiar with how Washington, D.C., works. He also relied on old friends in the media for advice, friends who would later turn on him in the worst of ways.

Unwittingly, Corey had a hand in the whole episode that ultimately helped Reince Priebus get the job.

Corey assumed the meeting he set up would be relatively predictable—one between Joe Scarborough, Mika Brzezinski, the daytime news talk show hosts, and Donald Trump in Trump Tower. Oddly enough, Scarborough had never met Steve Bannon and wanted to come in to see him and the president-elect so he could offer his advice. Corey couldn't have guessed how consequential those few minutes would be. During the meeting, Joe and Mika lobbied for Reince to become the chief of staff. They had also decided that Bannon would be much more effective if he took a role as some kind of senior advisor or senior strategist rather than the chief of staff position. We were as surprised as anyone that Steve was even willing to listen to their advice, given his avowed hatred for anyone who makes their living by being on television between the hours of six o'clock and noon on weekday mornings. These were the people he would usually refer to as "limousine liberals" or simply "the establishment." For Steve, having the approval of those media types was about as meaningful as a participation trophy.

And yet, somehow, when that meeting was over, the structure of the Trump White House had become clear. Joe and Mika helped convince the president-elect that Priebus should be the chief of staff, bringing along most of his team from the Republican National Committee. Steve Bannon would go into the building with the title "Chief Strategist" with a staff of one, refusing even to hire a secretary.

As Bannon and Priebus emerged as the two power brokers of Trump Tower, anyone who wanted a job in the administration had to go through them to get it.

Having Reince as chief of staff clearly had its benefits. First of all, he knew people and Washington, D.C. As head of the RNC, part of his job had been to work with members of Congress and the Senate to pass legislation. Bringing his people from the RNC made things a lot easier. Around Trump Tower, we began referring to this as the "plug-and-play" plan. He was simply moving his team from the RNC over to the White House, and that included the communications department, his senior staff, some mid-level assistants, and a few others. While this provided a temporary solution to the much-needed staffing hurdle, it also allowed the enemies to start destroying the administration from within.

There are multiple people who said negative things about the candidate during the campaign who ended up working in the White House. This doesn't mean they are enemies. For instance, Raj Shah called Trump "deplorable" on several occasions. After the *Access Hollywood* tape was released, Shah texted a fellow staffer at the RNC: "I'm kinda enjoying this, some justice. I honestly don't think it's the worst thing he's done but he somehow got passes for the other acts." Sean Spicer wanted Shah and within weeks he was doing final interviews to work in the White House.

On the other hand, Spicer was someone who had not been truly part of the Trump team. When we first asked him to help with the campaign, he refused. Actually, we both offered him a job. Corey asked him to join the campaign in March 2016 and he turned us down. When Mr. Trump became the Republican nominee, the RNC had little choice but show support, but when Dave offered him a job in June, he again said no. Only later would he come on board to help elect Mr. Trump, and even then it was reluctantly. After the first presidential debate, held at Hofstra University on Long Island, Spicer didn't want to go on camera during the media blitz in the spin room—a tradition that every press person does to talk up his candidate. Worst of all, however, just prior to election day, when the numbers were all against us, Spicer and others from the RNC did TV hits and private "off the record" conversations making excuses for Donald Trump's impending loss. Sean and his communications team brought a number of national reporters to the RNC the weekend before the election and told them the RNC was predicting a big loss for Trump.

After Mr. Trump's win, he had a change of heart. All of a sudden, he had some ideas about how to present Trump's message to the public—a message in which he had begun believing wholeheartedly, oddly enough, only after Donald Trump won the election.

To get the job, Sean didn't need to charm many of the right people. He and Reince worked closely together for years and Reince wanted and needed Sean in the building. With Sean overseeing the communications department, he was able to bring others from the November Ninth Club with him.

By the middle of December, Reince had earmarked Spicer to be the press secretary of the White House. Despite his refusal to join the campaign earlier, there seemed to be no lingering doubts that he would be moving into the building come January. Shortly before Christmas, the communications team was nearly fully staffed, but something like half of them had come straight from the RNC, while the other half came from the campaign. This set a dangerous precedent, and the damage it would create is still being felt in the White House today.

From the beginning, the boss had wanted Kellyanne Conway to play a major role in the communications department. But she had turned him down. Not unreasonably, Kellyanne believed that she would be able to serve the president better as counselor—a role that would allow her to have more input on policy and the general direction of the administration. On that point, she was correct. Kellyanne also wasn't keen on the idea of having to talk to the press every single day. For that, we couldn't blame her. During the campaign, no one had suffered the slings and arrows of the media more than Kellyanne Conway, with the exception of Donald J. Trump himself. Even when she out-argued and shut them down on the air, their sense of disrespect and hatred toward Donald Trump and, by extension her, was palpable. In the end, the boss understood her misgivings about taking on the role in the communications department and named her senior advisor and counselor to the president.

After Kellyanne, the president's favorites were Kimberly Guilfoyle, Laura Ingraham, or Monica Crowley, any of whom would have been quite a capable choice. You won't hear the media report that, of course, because it would disrupt their image of Trump as someone who doesn't respect strong women. Somehow all of these recommendations got lost in the shuffle. Reince entertained them, but it was clear he never really took them seriously. He wanted his people in key positions, and who could blame him? Because of Sean's duel role as communications director and press secretary, the communications staff never fully functioned correctly.

During that time, Corey took a trip to Mexico to visit Carlos Slim. He had become friendly with the billionaire's son during the campaign, and the Mexican telecommunications mogul had reached out to him hoping to meet with the president-elect. At his home in Mexico City, Slim suggested that Corey go to the Soumaya Museum, which Slim owns. The museum is spectacularly housed in a futuristically designed building. One of the exhibits displayed is a sculpture by Auguste Rodin. It consists of two colossal cast bronze doors at least fifteen feet high and is called the "Gates of Hell." Corey had someone take a photo of him standing in front of it. Then he texted the picture to Steve Bannon.

"Here's where we are," he wrote under the photo.

Little did he know just how prophetic the text would be—and how quickly the Deep State was going find its way through those gates.

Throughout much of the transition, the elevator doors at Trump Tower became very much like those bronze gates in the Rodin sculpture.

Still, by Christmas it seemed as if things would be pretty good for the new administration. The team was hiring good people, drafting good policy, and crafting an agenda to help the millions of people who had put the president-elect in office in the first place.

Hope Hicks joined the White House as the director of strategic communications, Keith Schiller went in as director of Oval Office operations, and Johnny McEntee went to work for the president as his body man. All great choices. Our friend Dan Scavino went inside as the director of social media and George Gigicos took over as director of advance. Andrew Giuliani went inside the administration to work in the Office of Public Liaison, the outreach arm of the White House to the business community.

Cassidy Dumbauld and Avi Berkowitz, both members of the campaign, went inside to help Jared Kushner. Stephen Miller entered government service as a senior advisor to the president.

Don McGahn, who served as the campaign attorney, was named White House counsel, and Peter Navarro went inside the government to help oversee trade policy for the president.

General Keith Kellogg joined the administration in a senior capacity as well. Additional campaign staff ended up in government agencies to ensure the president's agenda didn't get sidetracked. This included Joe Uddo, who ran Delaware for the campaign. He was hired to be the White House Liaison to the Department of Energy. Don Benton who served as our Washington State Chairman was appointed to head the Selective Service System under the Trump administration and Vincent DeVito from Massachusetts went to the Department of Interior as a Senior Advisor and Counsel to Secretary Ryan Zinke.

Still, the enemies of Trump were sneaking right through Rodin's gates every day.

On Christmas Day of 2016, Corey was taking a much-needed break with his family in Windham, New Hampshire. It had been a quiet day, without much news or word from Washington.

Corey and his wife, Alison, had been up since 4 a.m. to witness the usual Christmas morning carnage. Wrapping paper littered the floor in tatters; there were toys all over the room, and the kids were all laughing. For once, he wasn't thinking about politics—at least not as much as he usually does.

That evening, Alison's family came over for dinner. After they had cleared the table, the adults played cards, as they usually do. Texas hold 'em, quarter, half, and a dollar. Nobody gets hurt that way. Just as Corey was looking at his hand—which wasn't great, if he's remembering it correctly—his phone rang, which gave him an excuse to leave the table. As he made his way into the other room, Corey saw "Donald J. Trump" flash across the home screen of his phone.

He answered the call and heard the president-elect's voice on the other end. Trump said that he didn't want to talk business or politics, and that he had only called to say hello and wish Corey a Merry Christmas. They talked for a couple minutes—about the changes that were going on in both their lives, Corey's new business, the families, and how they had spent their holidays—and then Corey went to hang up the phone. He knew from watching Donald Trump how precious the president-elect's time with the family could be. He didn't want to take up any more of it than he already had.

After Corey said good-bye and was about to hang up the phone, Trump stopped him.

"Hold on," he said. "Let me say Merry Christmas to the kids."

Corey put the president-elect on speakerphone so the whole table could hear. Everyone in the room went quiet, obviously shocked to be hearing the future president of the United States in their kitchen. Donald Trump told the kids that they should be proud of their daddy, and that he wouldn't be where he was if it hadn't been for their father. To Corey, those words were a bit of a stretch. But they were still wonderful to hear.

When Trump was done, Corey hung up the phone and put it in his pocket. Then he walked out the back door and stood on the deck for a few moments by himself. He reflected briefly on the fact that Donald Trump was much more than a president to him. During the campaign, Corey had gotten much closer to the man than he'd been to just about anyone. Today, he's lucky to call him a friend and a mentor.

It was then that he knew that they might be able to keep him away from the White House, but they couldn't keep him away from helping the president.

CHAPTER 10

INSIDE THE WEST WING

IT WAS MID-FEBRUARY 2017 before Corey actually visited President Donald Trump in the White House. Up until then, Reince and many other establishment Republicans who staffed the West Wing had tried to block him from seeing the boss. He had talked with the president on the phone a few times since the inauguration, and in each conversation, President Trump had told Corey to make sure he came to see him. As you probably know, however, it's not that easy to just walk into the Oval Office and take a seat—it doesn't matter how well you know the president.

Many of the staff in the building didn't want Corey around because he believed in the philosophy of Let Trump Be Trump—while they believed they should "control" the president and make him more presidential. Some of the people making up the new administration, consisting of RNC-heavy staff and the Never-Trumpers, weren't part of the campaign and didn't likely vote for Trump on election day. They also did all they could to keep the president's friends out. Some of the staff thought Corey encouraged the president's worst instincts. The same instincts, by the way, that got him elected president—but these are minor details.

Finally, one night, after having spoken with the boss, Corey had had enough. He called Sean Spicer, saying the president had again asked for him to come in for a meeting and that some of the staff members who worked in the building were trying to block him. Sean told Corey that he would try to work something out, but that it would probably be a while before he could actually get inside. Things were tense, the boss was busy, there were wall-to-wall meetings—every excuse in the book.

"Listen," Corey said, "either you get me in to see him, or I'm going to blow you up on TV." Sean understood what that meant.

It was only after election day that Spicer had become a believer, another member of the November Ninth Club. In one passage of *The Briefing,* his White House memoir filled with inaccuracies, including calling the author of the phony Russian dossier Michael Steele (the once chairman of the Republican National Committee) instead of his correct name, Christopher Steele, Sean describes Donald Trump as a "unicorn, riding a unicorn over a rainbow."

We realized, however, that this wasn't just about us getting in to see the boss. Though the excuse the establishment Republicans used for walling off the president was that they wanted him to act "more presidential" (where have we heard that before?), what they really didn't want was anybody influencing the president away from their own agenda. We could see them trying to do that during the transition; however, we didn't realize how systemic the scheme had become in the White House.

A few hours after Corey ended the call with Spicer, his phone rang again. The screen looked odd. Instead of a name at the top, there was one line: the numbers "202" in bold on the top row, with Washington, D.C., in smaller font at the bottom. He was about to let it go to voice mail when he decided to pick up. It was Madeleine Westerhout, President Trump's personal secretary.

Madeleine and Corey confirmed noon the next day for his meeting with the president.

When Corey finally got in to see the president for the first time, Vice President Mike Pence joined them. It was a special moment. After a few minutes, before the vice president went off to give a speech, he asked Corey if he would bow his head and pray with him. When the vice president ended with the sign of the cross, Corey remembered thinking that if the Trump presidency was going to survive, it would need all the prayers it could get.

As adept as the establishment Republicans and the permanent Deep State were at sealing the White House off, they were that bad or worse at keeping information in. An administration springing leaks is nothing new, especially in a young administration that came to Washington, D.C., to be a change agent. They say that Benjamin Franklin was the first real leaker of the modern age. According to contemporaneous records, which are from long before the Revolutionary War, Franklin once got his hands on a

packet of letters from the governor of Massachusetts, his
rival, which contained proof that the governor was sympathetic to the British army. He kept them for a few days,
and then leaked them to his friend's newspaper by way of
a package left on the guy's doorstep. To this day, no one
knows who gave the letters to Franklin, or why.

Even Abraham Lincoln, our nation's first true
Republican president, had leaking proslavery Democrats
in his cabinet who sympathized with the Confederacy. The
first of the leaks was of Lincoln's State of the Union address,
which appeared in a New York paper before it was delivered
to Congress (by hand; it wasn't given in a speech then). But
the leak that almost sank the Lincoln presidency was about
his wife, Mary Todd, who had spent more money renovat-
ing the then shabby White House than she was supposed to.
The leak, though, had little to do with the expenditure. The
leakers were people who thought Lincoln wanted too much
power, and that he didn't rely enough on the government
employees in his midst to get things done. It's funny how
that motivation hasn't changed in all these years.

Leaking in the White House has continued throughout
the ages. Mostly those leaks contained only small bits of
meeting minutes and documents that were under the review
process. Only on rare occasions would full transcripts or
whole packages of documents leak—the Pentagon Papers,
for instance. And when that did happen, people went to
court over it. Even the most ardent supporters of a free
press knew that the executive branch couldn't run without some degree of privacy. It's part of the reason there
are gates in front of the White House and thick, multilay-
ered metal walls around the Situation Room. Sometimes
secrecy is necessary.

But when Donald Trump took office, everything changed. Thanks to the hysterical Fake News led by left-wing agitators who were constantly creating made-up allegations, people were being told that the president was unhinged, crazy, or that he had some form of dementia. The media painted him as some tyrannical figure who wanted to crown himself dictator, the same way people thought about Lincoln during the Civil War. The reasons for the leaks spanned the spectrum from those who thought they were patriots and were saving the country, to those whose motives were purely self-serving, like those of Reality Winner, a convicted felon who leaked classified documents in an attempt to hurt President Trump. There were others, too, who just didn't know any better and were scared for their jobs, which, in many cases, they should have been. At one time, these people could hope to hold their positions for life without the possibility of ever being fired. Donald Trump came to Washington to change all that.

So, by January 2017, there were people on the inside, as close as in the West Wing, who were looking to cripple the presidency. The only question was—and still is—who were they?

The first leaks had occurred early, before the White House furniture the first lady picked out even arrived. They were small things that any new administration should expect—details of meetings about staff positions, cabinet conversations, and short pronouncements from the president, most of which had been given in front of large groups of staffers. These were the kinds of leaks we could deal with; they were just part of running the government.

On August 3, 2017, something extraordinary happened.

Pieces of a transcript of President Trump's private conversation with Malcolm Turnbull, the then prime minister of Australia, were leaked right after their phone call to the *Washington Post*. This was a new kind of leak. It was immediate and seemed to have been initiated for the purpose of making the president look bad.

The call had been made on a White House line—the same one that previous presidents had used for years to conduct official government business with other world leaders without a hint of a leak—one where there is not only assumption of confidentiality for both parties but almost a guarantee. This gave the president and the prime minister freedom to say things to each other that they probably wouldn't want to be printed in the newspapers—things that are often necessary for tough negotiations.

According to a few of our sources in the administration, there is really only one way this could have happened other than some outside hacker who found his or her way into the White House switchboard and secretly recorded the call, which didn't take place. The calls that come through the White House switchboard system are not like cell phone calls—they can't be snatched from the air in the way personal phone calls from our cell phones can.

What makes it even more unlikely is that the call itself wasn't exactly about state secrets or nuclear missiles. Instead, it was meant to be an hour-long introductory conversation about trade and diplomacy, the details of which would be so dull they wouldn't have made it into a spy novel.

Sources say a strong possibility is that someone under the direction of Prime Minister Turnbull leaked it. However, the most likely scenario is that someone on the inside of the West Wing—one of the few people with access to the president's phone line—either took notes while listening to the call or secretly recorded the whole thing. By "someone," of course, we don't mean the person whose job it is to make a record of the phone call. Those people are well vetted, and "unimpeachable," according to one of our sources. Theirs is an important job that allows us to preserve a record of the Trump presidency for historians and political scientists of the future.

What we mean is people who may be listening from other areas of the building. Calls to the president are connected through the White House switchboard and desk officers in the Situation Room can listen in on these conversations anytime they want even though they're not supposed to. The connections are made through them and they just stay on the line in silent mode. These are people in the NSC or CIA, many of whom are holdovers from the Obama administration, with far too much access to the computer systems and phone lines of the White House.

So why does someone whose real job is to arrange meetings and type up notes for their bosses have access to classified documents? We wondered the same thing, and here's what we found out. Not surprisingly, the answer has to do with a disastrous decision made by the Obama administration.

In George W. Bush's White House, if you wanted to, say, order a drone strike, you probably had to do the following: have a meeting, type up some kind of order, print it out, show it to someone, then talk about it, then retype it with corrections, show it to someone else, get some more notes, carry it around to the different department heads, then get notes from them, and so on, and so on. By the end of that process, you might have lost your itch to bomb something! This, as you might imagine, is something the Obama team wouldn't stand for. The central tenet of their foreign policy was that White House basement-office dwellers like Ben Rhodes had the right to take massive action whenever they felt like it. Career public servants also had a say and didn't have to go through any type of pesky approval process.

When the Obama team took over, the internet hadn't quite taken over the White House. Briefings were still done almost entirely on paper, and speeches were even typed up, printed out, and edited by hand. This meant that people at the top made most of the decisions in small rooms, in small groups, and very little of the information ever got out of those rooms. If you're Barack Obama, who liked to leave the big decisions up to his twenty-something-year-old staff members, this was a problem.

So they instituted a file-sharing software system called "SharePoint," which allowed more people than ever to access classified documents. Instead of working on things from separate computers and emailing them around, people would now create documents in a shared space—to which about three hundred people had unrestricted access—and make corrections as a community. This system could be accessed by just about everyone in the National Security Council, at any time, from any place in the building.

This meant that when something leaked from the SharePoint, it could have come from any one of about three hundred people who had access to the document.

The main problem with this new system is that there was no way of tracing who had seen what. People were identified by their computer terminals, so anyone could take a peek at the screen, copy down what they saw, then log off. Anyone could do it on H. R. McMaster's computer, for instance, and no one would ever know what they had seen. It is this kind of snooping, according to our sources in the White House, that allowed the first leak of President Trump's call with the Australian prime minister.

Allegedly, it was holdovers of the Obama administration—people who had worked in the basement offices and government agencies and then secretly lobbied people like Ben Rhodes and Susan Rice to keep their jobs for a few months—who did most of the early leaking. There are those who believe these holdovers' actions are laudable because they were doing something good for their country. It's bullshit. Not only does it dismiss the will of the people who voted for Donald Trump for the presidency, but it's a fundamental lie. What they did, and continue to do, is not about saving the country. It's about holding on to power. Donald Trump is the biggest threat to the status quo and administrative state since Abraham Lincoln. The bureaucrats weren't about to give up without a fight.

The next round of leaks—the ones that would download full-length transcripts off the cloud server and give them in full to newspapers all over the country—would show just how far they were willing to go to make President Trump look bad.

Just one month into his term, the press was already running stories wondering if the president would last a year. The West Wing was leaking so badly it should have been wearing an adult diaper. Those leaks went from the absurd (the president goes to the residence at 6:30 p.m.

and changes into his bathrobe) to ones that risked national security, like what the president said to foreign leaders in the Oval Office.

Outside the White House, a headwind of obstructionists and haters had already begun to organize. Those headwinds would get stronger by the day. Just that week Obama's political guru, David Axelrod, invited Corey to speak at the Institute of Politics at the University of Chicago. His appearance drew the ire of a faction of students. Protests erupted outside the venue. The day of Corey's speech, students hung an effigy of the president outside the building where he was supposed to be speaking. Protesters egged on their children to beat the effigy with bats until the head was separated and the rest was in pieces.

Within months the hate would be blowing at hurricane strength. Celebrities like Meryl Streep, Chelsea Handler, and Robert De Niro spewed vile remarks against the president. The press that had been hateful toward Donald Trump became weaponized against him. Those inside the White House, the staff that was supposed to protect the president, either cowered or leaked to the press—or worse. At least on the outside you knew who Trump's enemies were. Inside, they weren't that easy to identify.

Over the next twelve months, the West Wing changed dramatically. But even the revolving door couldn't slow the president's agenda.

The president fired his first chief of staff, Reince Priebus, via tweet on July 28, 2017. That day President Trump had traveled with his chief of staff to a fund-raiser in Long Island. The president sent the tweet just before he deplaned Air Force One at Joint Base Andrews upon their return. Reince knew that it was coming for some time. He said nothing to reporters as he made his way across the tarmac in the heavy rain. Reince was thrust into a no-win situation, with too many forces vying for the control of access to the president to be successful.

Reince had previously served as the chairman of the RNC and reported to the 168 members of the committee; in essence he didn't have a boss. He was great at fund-raising and voter turnout but running the White House required a different skill set. It was a pressure-filled environment where decisions are made on a minute-by-minute basis, decisions that impact the rest of the world.

Reince knew this as well as anyone, which is why he brought Katie Walsh with him into the White House as his deputy chief of staff. Walsh had been the RNC chief of staff under Reince and earned a reputation as a no-nonsense professional. In addition to being the chief of staff, her role was as the conduit between the RNC and the Trump campaign. Katie was one of the first senior staffers to depart the White House. In March 2017, GotNews, a conservative blog, ran a story identifying Walsh as the leaker in the White House. That blog post then somehow found its way onto the *Drudge Report,* where it was read by everybody.

When she departed the White House, Reince was left without his advocate in a place where advocates are hard to find.

The president replaced Reince with homeland security secretary and retired four-star Marine general John F. Kelly as the new White House chief of staff. As far as we know, the decision was unilateral on the president's part. He had had it with the leaks and negative press that flowed from the White House, mostly because it obscured all the things his administration was accomplishing.

The president promoted Kelly to defeat the false narrative that the White House was in disarray. He also wanted someone who would lock down the leaks. If you're looking for someone who will command respect, picking a retired four-star general is a solid choice. General Kelly told the president that he would take the job only if everyone, and he meant everyone, even family, would report to him.

The president agreed, and John Kelly assumed the chief of staff position.

The first thing Kelly did after being sworn in was fire Anthony Scaramucci for his well-documented meltdown with a *New Yorker* reporter.

Kelly also brought in Kirstjen Nielsen to serve as his principal deputy chief of staff. She served in a similar role with Kelly at the Department of Homeland Security. Neither Kelly nor Nielsen had any political experience and their interactions with the Fake News had also been fairly limited. One of the first things Kelly did was attempt to control access to the president. In our opinion, he believed President Trump was a tiger that needed to be caged and kept from anyone who Kelly believed would throw him red meat.

Very early in the 2016 presidential campaign, back when Corey still shared an office with Sam Nunberg on the twenty-fourth floor of Trump Tower, back when you could count the number of people working on Trump's campaign with one hand, Corey took out a Magic Marker and wrote four words on the whiteboard in the office. Those words became the mantra of the campaign, and part of the reason Trump connected with people from across all spectrums. Those words were some of the reasons why he won the election, and why he had the promise to be a transformative president. Those words were, "Let Trump Be Trump." Yet, throughout his brief political career, the boss has been surrounded by people who, because of their own beliefs, have tried to make him into something he isn't.

Over the next few months, things in the West Wing got marginally better. There were still leaks, such as when the full transcripts of the president's calls in January to Mexican president Peña Nieto and Prime Minister Malcolm Turnbull were leaked to the *Washington Post* in August 2017. In October, a memo by Tom Bossert, President Trump's homeland security advisor, concerning the hurricane in Puerto Rico was leaked to Axios.

The Fake News painted Kelly as the disciplinarian the West Wing needed, and the man who keeps an eye on the president to protect the nation. "Kelly tightens his grip on the West Wing," wrote the *Hill*; "New Chief of Staff Kelly Moves Quickly to Tame Trump's Tweets," shouted Bloomberg; "John Kelly's Latest Mission: Controlling the Information Flow to Trump," said the *New York Times*.

What the media continuously fails to recognize is that Donald Trump is the boss.

On September 19, 2017, the president addressed the United Nations General Assembly for the first time. It was in that address that he called the North Korean ruler, Kim Jong Un, "Rocket Man." While diplomats and journalists where scratching their heads wondering how the president had come up with that phrase, we had flashbacks to our time on Trump Force One listening to Elton John. After a heated Twitter exchange between the two leaders, the president added "little" to the title, and Kim was "Little Rocket Man" to the whole world.

Aides, including, according to Bob Woodward's book, Rob Porter and others, tried to get the president to tone down his tweets, worried that the war of words would escalate. However, Trump knew exactly what he was doing. "You have to show some strength," the president reportedly said.

He would get the chance to do just that.

When Kim became threatening, the president shot this tweet back: "North Korean Leader Kim Jong Un just stated that the Nuclear Button is on his desk at all times," Trump wrote on Twitter at 7:49 p.m.

"Will someone from his depleted and food starved regime please inform him that I too have a Nuclear Button, but it is a much bigger & more powerful one than his, and my Button works!"

The main stream media and liberal left almost exploded. Pundits from every big news organization screamed to high heavens: "He's going to get us into a nuclear war!!"

As it turned out, the opposite was true. The president had known exactly what he was doing. He tweeted, "I told Rex Tillerson, our wonderful Secretary of State, that he is wasting his time trying to negotiate with Little Rocket Man. Save your energy Rex, we'll do what has to be done!"

President Trump went with his instincts, and those instincts knew how to handle Kim, and a few months later they met in a historic summit in Singapore, which has brought us closer to complete nuclear disarmament on the Korean Peninsula and has made the world a safer place.

In December, the president went from unprecedented international diplomacy to a sweeping and historic tax reform bill, which put more money in the pockets of hardworking American men and women and brought more "jobs, jobs, jobs," as the president said, to the American workforce.

And he was able to show such mastery on both the international and domestic fronts in spite of the fact that his own staff was actively trying to thwart his agenda and presidential style.

The president's former staff secretary, Rob Porter, had an exemplary résumé and the bloodlines to match. He went to both Harvard and Oxford. His father, Roger Porter, a professor at Harvard, worked for three Republican administrations, including Reagan's. If you looked up the words "establishment Republican" in the dictionary, Rob Porter's picture would be alongside the definition. In other words, he was never a good fit to work on the America First agenda. But he was brought in as gatekeeper of the Oval Office and given the charge of keeping an eye on the president. He did a lot more than keep an eye on Donald Trump. Along with Gary Cohn and Anonymous, the cowardly author of the *New York Times* op-ed, Rob Porter thought his job was to control information and access to the president, thereby making him more "presidential."

It wasn't his sins as what Anonymous referred to as the "steady state," however, that got him fired. No, it was something that you might not have guessed considering his clean-cut image.

Porter's White House career ended in ignominy. The *Daily Mail* online was the first to publish allegations of his spousal abuse.

Two of his ex-wives came forward to say that he abused them. One wrote about the abuse in the *Washington Post*.

The article ran under a photo of her with a black eye. The allegations certainly seemed credible.

Instead of firing Porter on the spot, however, General Kelly initially sang Porter's praises. "I can't say enough good things about him," Kelly said publicly. "He is a friend, a confidant, and a trusted professional. I am proud to serve alongside him." He would go on to say that Porter was a man of integrity and true honor.

Porter's ex-wives would not agree. Here's what one had to say about Porter in the *Washington Post*: "For me, living in constant fear of Rob's anger and being subjected to his degrading tirades for years chipped away at my independence and sense of self-worth. I walked away from that relationship a shell of the person I was when I went into it . . . "

Upon publication of these interviews, along with the photographs, General Kelly expedited Rob Porter's departure from the White House.

More problems, and bigger enemies, however, awaited the president on Capitol Hill.

CHAPTER 11

ENEMIES IN CONGRESS

FOR ABOUT TWO YEARS AFTER the Clinton team came up with the fake collusion narrative, Republicans in the House of Representatives conducted hearings on Russia. They interviewed everyone who was even tangentially involved in the Trump campaign—from the lowest of the low-level campaign staff to the friends and family of the candidate himself, looking for evidence of any ties to Russia at all. By April of 2018, they had found absolutely nothing, and there was only one witness left to interview: Corey.

After testifying once for eight hours, he finally agreed to come in again and answer questions before the committee. He began the interview by saying that he would only answer "relevant" questions. But this didn't stop the panel from hounding him for information about everything they could think of. The questions went on for hours before Corey finally decided things had gone on long enough.

After repeating several times that he wouldn't be answering questions on what happened after he left the campaign, Corey delivered a somewhat blunt message, which made a few headlines: "I'm not answering any of your fucking questions about what happened after I left," he said.

Since then, they haven't called him back to testify. But Democrats in Congress have dragged many people in who aren't as plainspoken as Corey, torturing them for hours with questions about Russia and their fake collusion story. They have also continued to block every policy that Donald Trump puts forward, and to attack the president at every opportunity. Enemies of Trump have all but taken over Congress, and they present an enormous danger to the America First agenda.

Broadly speaking, the enemies of President Trump in Congress fall into two categories. In the first, we have activists who will never have a nice word to say about a booming economy, tax cuts, and a safer America. These congressmen and senators are constantly quoted in "news" stories and are a constant presence on the Never-Trump networks. In the second category, we have the "quiet band," including both Democrats and a handful of squishy Republicans who are behind the scenes sabotaging the Trump agenda in the congressional shadows. Both of these groups of politicians are doing all they can to resist Trump's policies for all the wrong reasons.

In the Senate, Democrats with an eye on the White House have created Fake News to oppose President Trump's nominees to the Supreme Court and the federal bench, even though President Trump has made historic strides to nominate qualified jurists who follow the text of the Constitution. You can't change the channel on your television without hearing the stump speech of a Trump-hating senator campaigning for 2020. The Trump list of accomplishments is long, yet these many victories for middle America come despite resistance from establishment forces in his own party and a reflexive opposition by all Democrats to every element of the Trump agenda to Make America Great Again. They don't want greatness—they want mediocrity and they want to regain power at all costs.

The most pernicious of Trump's opponents are trying to game the Constitution to overturn the 2016 election. Some on the left claim that Trump did not win the last election and others are trying to make the case that somehow the president has triggered impeachment proceedings. They hate him and his pro-freedom agenda, which puts America first and foreign interests last. Liberal Democrats hate putting Americans first, because they consider themselves members of a global interest group where collectivism is embraced and capitalism is hated. These "America last" politicians look to Europeans for ideas on how to impose socialism on America while forcing American taxpayers to pay for the defense of other nations' borders.

Publicity-seeking representative Adam Schiff (D-CA) has used his position as ranking member of the House Permanent Committee on Intelligence to leverage millions in earned media hits. One way he has garnered attention is to leak the contents of closed-door hearings, including the testimony of Corey R. Lewandowski in March 2018. Schiff has promised to use the next Congress to investigate alleged funneling of Russian money into the Trump organization. Ironically, this is the same Adam Schiff who ignores the real scandal of Russians funneling money into the Clinton Foundation. Only a partisan hack could justify the obvious double standard.

Schiff has not called for hearings into the Uranium One scandal, where there are multiple reports that the Russians funneled money into the Clinton Foundation to purchase favors from the Obama administration via Secretary of State Hillary Clinton. The Russian government had taken over a Canadian mining company to corner the market on uranium mining from Asia to the United States for the purposes of controlling new mining. This is a real scandal, yet partisan hack Schiff called the Hillary–Uranium One scandal an "orchestrated distraction." One would think that Schiff is a selfless speaker of the truth the way he talks about the Trump investigations, yet he clams up and distracts attention from the real Russian conspiracy scandal to corner the world market in uranium mining with the help of Democrat Hillary Clinton. Schiff is a committed partisan who sees no evil in anything a Democrat does, even when it might lead to the Russians getting more nuclear material.

The very liberal *New York Times* reported on April 23, 2015, that "at the heart of the tale are several men, leaders of the Canadian mining industry, who have been major donors to the charitable endeavors of former President Bill Clinton and his family. Members of that group built, financed, and eventually sold off to the Russians a company that would become known as Uranium One." According to the story, while the Russians slowly took over Uranium One, the chairman of the company funneled $2.35 million in secret donations to the foundation, despite Clinton's agreement to disclose all contributions to the Clinton Foundation after she took office. Clinton was part of a team of administration officials who signed off on the Russians taking control over American uranium. Schiff would rather chase ghosts and allege nonexistent ties between Russians and Donald Trump to drum up more media interviews.

Schiff didn't merely turn a blind eye to the Uranium One scandal; he also was complicit in covering up the failures of Hillary's war in Libya. Schiff carried the partisan water for the Obama administration and Hillary's failure in Libya when he called Benghazi security officers liars for telling the story of failed security at the American CIA Annex in Libya leading to the deaths of Americans stationed abroad. Schiff can't be trusted, because he has proven to take partisan marching orders to spread disinformation and lies when it serves his party's purposes.

Some enemies have even used congressional hearings to leverage anonymous leaks and cable TV commentary to commence informal impeachment proceedings to toss the president out of office. One of the more obnoxious antagonists is Representative Eric Swalwell (D-CA), who is considering a run for President. He has been one of the loudest calling for hearings into every aspect of the Trump 2016 campaign. It is no coincidence that Swalwell has made ten trips to Iowa since President Trump was sworn in, to set the table for a run against the president in 2020. The congressman has used his position on the House Permanent Select Committee on Intelligence and Judiciary to beat up a political foe.

Swalwell is very ambitious and a hard-core leftist. He challenged and defeated a well-respected incumbent, Democrat representative Pete Stark, in 2012, because Swalwell could not wait for the twenty-term incumbent to retire from his seat in Congress. Since being elected to

Congress, this man with an eye on the White House has recorded a video of himself voting to allow late-term abortions and has penned an op-ed in *USA Today* advocating mandatory gun confiscation. It should not be a surprise that Swalwell is a House leader of the movement to beat President Trump in 2020 by using constant oversight hearings over the next two years. These hearings would help Swalwell with his long-shot bid for president.

Guys like Swalwell whisper about impeachment, so they can make believe they care about good policy. He was on MSNBC to make the case to Never-Trump Republican Nicole Wallace in August 2018 that Democrats should wait until after the election to push for impeachment, because they don't yet have a majority. Swalwell, a constant arrogant annoyance on cable TV, has been very critical of the president and loves to hear his own voice on why endless hearings are necessary. The media loves him because he is one of those politicians who never has a nice word to say about President Trump.

Not surprisingly, Swalwell has not been free from his own scandal. One of the first acts he took when elected to Congress was to hire the daughter of a wealthy donor to his campaign. In addition, Swalwell has been a loyal supporter of his fellow Californian House minority leader Nancy Pelosi, even though his politics should lead him to team up with the Democrat Socialist wing of the party. Yet, Swalwell's loyalty is expected to be rewarded with cash donations for his presidential run when he announces. Swalwell has fit like a glove into the D.C. swamp with his boundless ambition, constant media appearances, and his embrace of cronyism.

Another left-wing product of the People's Republic of

California is crazy Democrat representative Maxine Waters, who is the most aggressive advocate for evidence-free impeachment of the president. She also frequently calls for violence and harassment against Trump supporters and government officials. If Waters were not such a cartoonish version of a liberal Democrat, she would be higher up on the list of the enemies of Trump. Hardly any members of Congress, and even fewer American citizens, take Waters' rants seriously, yet the media can't get enough of her crazy calls for violence and impeachment. Need to entertain some of the looney left who cling to their lattes and MSNBC? Book crazy Maxine Waters for an entertaining rant about Trump. Some laugh with her, but most laugh at her bizarre appearances.

Waters has become the angry face of the Democrat Party during President Trump's first term in office. As recently as September 2018, Waters pledged to "get him" when referring to President Trump. The congresswoman then went on a whacky rant where she responded to a question about Democrats' reluctance to say the word "impeachment" by saying "impeachment, impeachment, impeachment, impeachment, impeachment, impeachment, impeachment." Sneaky Democrats like Swalwell whisper about impeachment, while the crazy, and honest ones, scream the word from the rooftops.

When not yelling about toppling President Trump from power, Waters has called for harm to his supporters. On June 25, 2018, RealClearPolitics posted a video of Waters saying that "God is on our side" and "if you see anybody from that Cabinet in a restaurant, in a department store, at a gasoline station, you get out and you form a crowd and you push back on them and you tell them 'you are not welcome' anymore—anywhere." Democrats are now invoking religion to push for a holy war against Trump supporters that likely will incite violence. The same politicians who want to pass federal laws criminalizing speech that is not politically correct are the ones setting the table with hateful rhetoric for violence against proud supporters of Donald J. Trump and his administration.

The enemies of President Trump find, alas, that their angry obsession does not allow them a moment of personal happiness. When Waters celebrated her eightieth birthday, she didn't make it a happy occasion. Waters is so blinded with hate that she announced her birthday wish was for President Trump's impeachment this past August. When many eighty-year-old seniors are making time to visit with kids and grandchildren, Waters is having a cake baked with hate and celebrated with a call to knock the president out of office. Crazy and sick with rage, this unbalanced elderly politician has pushed herself to become the new-yet-old face of the Democrat Party.

Another hater of the president is the elected leader of the House Democrats, Nancy Pelosi. The liberal San Francisco pillar is one of the politicians running point on the fight to stop the Trump agenda, yet she has proven to be a shaky and ineffective spokeswoman for the enemies of President Trump. Pelosi can't even round up support within her own Democrat caucus for her leadership skills. When not stumbling to find a word, Pelosi has fallen into the lazy habit of calling the president racially insensitive. Pelosi accused Trump of engaging "in it [racism] constantly." It is disgraceful that a leader of the Democrats would use name calling to disparage our president.

Pelosi wants President Trump to fail so badly that she

has become a cheerleader for an economic depression. When numbers were released in the middle of 2018 that showed consumer confidence at the highest number in decades and unemployment rates at a historic low, Pelosi argued, "[P]eople say: Oh my goodness . . . people are saying the unemployment rate is down, why isn't my purchasing power increasing? So, this isn't just about the unemployment rate, it's about wages rising in our country, so that consumer confidence is restored." Facts don't matter to progressives who hate everything about President Trump. They can't give him any credit for a booming economy and have to make believe that good news is bad news.

When Dave was working as investigator on the Whitewater committee, he spent much of his time with the chairman of the committee, the legendary senator from New York, Alfonse D'Amato. Sometimes Dave would accompany the senator to floor votes. One of the first times he did, D'Amato told him to wait in the cloakroom off the Senate floor. Dave was fairly new to ways of the U.S. Senate, so he didn't know the cloakroom was for the use of senators only. A couple of the staffers asked him to leave and he did.

At the time, Dave was working sixteen-hour days, seven days a week for the committee. The next time he accompanied Senator D'Amato to the Senate chamber, the cloakroom with its big leather chairs looked too comfortable to pass up. He sat down and within seconds he nodded off. The next thing he remembers was being awoken by a staffer laughing at him.

In the months that followed, the Whitewater team would conduct an aggressive investigation utilizing dozens of subpoenas as well as nearly a hundred depositions. Over the course of his political career, Dave has come to know Capitol Hill as well as anyone. In fact, both of us have worked in the House and the Senate, and we believe that the worst obstructionists are in the Senate.

The Senate contains its share of the enemies of Trump. For example, Senator Cory Booker (D-NJ) has had his sights on the presidency for a long, long time and he is using his opposition to everything Trump to drum up support. Booker was so desperate for good press back when he was mayor of Newark, New Jersey, he created an imaginary friend and foe "T-Bone," who both threatened Booker's life and cried on his shoulder. Whenever Booker told a heroic story about him stopping street gangs or saving kids from the streets, Booker's imaginary friend T-Bone would somehow show up in the story. *National Review* reported:

> "But sources tell National Review Online that the central character in one of Booker's oft-repeated stories—T-Bone, the drug pusher who the mayor has said threatened his life at one turn and sobbed on his shoulder the next—is a figment of his imagination, even though Booker has talked about him in highly emotional terms and in great detail."

Booker, who aspires to be the next Democrat to lose to President Trump in a general election, has imaginary friends. It is scary that somebody who creates a fake person for the purposes of telling stories is being relied on by the left and the mainstream media as a credible critic of the president.

President Barack Obama's favorite politician, Senator Kamala Harris (D-CA), is another enemy of President Trump who is campaigning hard to use the power of

Congress to forward her campaign for president. Senator Harris got her first big break in politics in 1994 when she started dating California Assembly Speaker Willie Brown and he had her appointed to a no-show job with the California Medical Assistance Commission. Senator Harris only had to attend one meeting a month and made about $72,000 a year. What a great way to become a feminist hero by using a relationship with an elderly, powerful man to get ahead. When Harris preaches about women's rights and tries to become the first woman president of the United States, it will not be ignored that the first big boost Harris had in her career was not on her merit as a competent attorney.

Harris has some dubious views on the Constitution and seems to ignore the fact that the president has the power under Article II, Section 2 of the U.S. Constitution to issue pardons. In August of this year, Senator Harris falsely stated that the presidential constitutional power to pardon would constitute the crime of obstruction of justice under certain circumstances. The left loves to create new crimes and tries to limit the power of the president's Article II power to pardon and to run the executive branch of the federal government.

Not to be outdone is many people's favorite liberal wacko, Senator Elizabeth Warren (D-MA). When not defending her alleged Native American heritage, Senator Warren has been working hard to get ready to fight Trump for the next two years. President Trump likes to call her "Pocahontas" Warren because she has created the false impression that she is Native American. It was reported, "Harvard Law School in the 1990s touted Warren, then a professor in Cambridge, as being 'Native American.'"

They singled her out, Warren later acknowledged, because she had listed herself as a minority in an Association of American Law Schools directory. Critics note that she had not done that in her student applications and during her time as a teacher at the University of Texas. Appropriating Native American heritage is a sign of a person desperate to use membership in a minority group for political gain. Warren is an enemy of the president who needs to apologize to Native American people for stealing their identity. She makes no claim about growing up on a reservation, nor any real ties to the Native American community, just that she remembers her mother saying something about her heritage generations ago. Senator Warren should always be introduced by the media as the senator who appropriated Native American heritage before they allow her to rant about her many critiques of President Trump. Ironically, President Trump is just as Native American as "Fauxcahontas" Elizabeth Warren, the Democrat faux Native American.

Senator Warren is an older breed of the Democrat socialists who have recently emerged as the ideological leaders of the party. There is not a regulatory idea or a new tax that Warren has not embraced as she advocates for massive new spending on government-run health care and free college tuition for all. Warren has allied herself with the socialist ideas of Senator Bernie Sanders (I-VT), who wants the American economy to look more like Venezuela or North Korea. They voice opposition to tax cuts, lower unemployment numbers, and a booming Trump economy while calling for a massive government takeover of the private economy to steal from the job-creating companies so the politicians can spend it.

There are many more Democrats who make this list of enemies of President Trump. Senator Jeff Merkley (D-OR) is one of them. Merkley was profiled by the *New York Times* in June in the midst of many early trips to Iowa to plant the seed for a run against Trump. They described him as a senator who has "not been a legislative standout, and is known mostly as the only senator who endorsed Mr. Sanders over Hillary Clinton in the 2016 Democrat presidential primaries." Trump supporters can thank Merkley for being a champion for changes to the filibuster that helped President Trump load up the federal courts with great jurists. Unwittingly, Merkley is a big advocate of getting rid of the filibuster in a way that would help President Trump pass even more tax cuts and repeal Obamacare. Of course, Merkley advocated these positions when he was under the influence of the mistaken belief that Democrats would storm to victory in all branches of government in the last election. One should expect that Merkley has had a change of heart on this issue for purely partisan reasons.

There are a handful of Republicans who falsely thought that being Never-Trump politicians would help them. Politics works when there is a healthy fight between disagreeing parties and when those politicians can put aside nasty language and differences when they have a common interest. Look at Senators Rand Paul (R-KY), Ted Cruz (R-TX), Marco Rubio (R-FL), and Lindsey Graham (R-SC) as examples of politicians who fought hard and used hard-edged rhetoric to fight, and lose, to President Trump. All of these Republican primary opponents put aside some hard feelings to not only get along with the president, but to become his defenders against the enemies in Congress.

The meek Republican members of the Senate who oppose the president in the shadows are the ones who are now the loudest while exiting politics. Some Republicans who were not brave enough to run against Trump for president are among the loudest enemies of the president. That group includes Senators Bob Corker (R-TN), Ben Sasse (R-NE), and Jeff Flake (R-AZ), of which only Sasse will be coming back for a few more years. It is hard to imagine that Sasse would even bother to run in 2020 on a ticket with incumbent president Donald J. Trump on the top of the ticket, because he will look at polls and rightly assume that he can't win a primary for his own seat. Never-Trump Republicans are facing tough times within the party—and for good reason. Most of them are looking for lobbying or consulting jobs in the D.C. swamp after they leave Congress.

Senator Flake has become the leader of that group of Never-Trump senators who were early opponents of the president. Flake has become the elected Republican face of both the Never-Trump movement within the Republican Party and the poster child for how to ruin a political career—in his case his own. Once a promising rebel member of the House of Representatives, Flake was absorbed into the establishment upon his election to the Senate in 2013. For some reason, Flake thought it good politics to toss all his political chips into the Never-Trump movement. Not a senator who was known for brave stands on legislation or doing much of anything, Flake made the political calculation that being against Trump was good for his future. Boy, was he wrong.

When it was time for the Trump-hating Flake to decide whether to run for his Senate seat again, Flake looked at his abysmal 18 percent approval rating and polls indicating that he was a lock to lose, and decided to hang up the cleats. The lesson learned was that Republicans love President Trump and Democrats will never embrace Never-Trump Republican politicians when they can elect Democrat socialists who will take the fight to the next level. Jeff Flake is a case study in how a squishy Republican politician can take a blowtorch to his or her career by joining the small band of RINOs in the Republican Party who make a living of opposing President Donald J. Trump. Republicans against Trump has become a cottage industry, and even some retired members are trying to break through with media careers by trashing the president.

In the House, Representative Carlos Curbelo (R-FL) is the example of a House member who engaged in political treason for personal gain. He has fallen for the fallacy that if you are a Republican supporting Trump's impeachment, Democrats and liberal independents will love you. Curbelo plunged the political knife in the back of the Trump administration when he had his staff call a far-left wing publication, *Mother Jones*, to make sure they gave him credit for being the first Republican to call for impeachment hearings on the leader of his own party. Curbelo was motivated to act like a Democrat because his district voted for Hillary Clinton over Donald Trump by 16.3 percent. Curbelo is hardly a profile in courage and is a great example of a Republican who has ruined his career by becoming the Democrat-lite version of the Republican Party that so many American voters hate.

Democratic representatives like Schiff, Swalwell, Waters, and Pelosi are unhinged and hypocritical. They are losers in politics and the American people understand that they have it out for the president. They want to impeach the president in the House to start the process of beating up President Trump's reputation and to stall his conservative agenda. Then there are senators such as Booker, Warren, Harris, and Merkley who fully understand that impeachment is a means to an end—they want to create doubt in the American people's minds about President Trump so one of them can sneak into the White House to impose a Democrat socialist agenda full of taxpayer and middle-class-funded free health care for all, free tuition for college, and government-funded green energy programs to line the pockets of left-wing contributors like Tom Steyer. The Republican traitors to their own party have miscalculated, because as much as hard-core left-wing voters hate Trump and all Republicans, Trump support among the party's voters is at a historic high. The Jeff Flake wing of the party will be effectively flipping burgers on the street before you know it.

President Trump's enemies have proven to be a bunch of losers—literally.

Either they retired like senators Jeff Flake and Bob Corker before they were tossed aside by Republican primary voters or they became hated by a base of the Republican Party that loves the president. The enemies of Trump have proven to be a bit crazy and full of baloney, with some political turncoats mixed in. There are some enemies of Trump who have truly evil motives. They aim to use Congress to remove a duly elected president. Let them try, but the American people will use the most powerful tool at their disposal—the power to vote—to make sure that the enemies of Trump will never be allowed to win.

CHAPTER 12

THE ADMINISTRATIVE STATE

SINCE DONALD TRUMP was elected, we've spent every spare minute helping forward the president's America First agenda, supporting those in Congress who supported it, and helping fight off Trump's enemies where we could. We spend a lot of time on TV—you might have seen us.

Both of us have day jobs, however. Dave is the president of the nonprofit conservative political organization Citizens United. This organization is famous for the 2010 Supreme Court decision that would rewrite campaign finance law by protecting free speech and the First Amendment.

Corey did some consulting with a partner for a couple of months after the election, but he wasn't happy. The Fake News descended on him like vultures.

The attack by the press came in spite of the fact that Corey had made it clear from the start that he was not a lobbyist. The last thing he was going to do was to trade on his friendship with the president. He would have set fire to his office in five minutes if he thought even one of his clients might not support the president's America First agenda.

When word hit the streets of D.C. that he had gone into the consulting business, Corey was deluged with calls and opportunities. The majority of them were candidates and companies looking to grow and use some of what he had learned on the Trump campaign to better understand how the Trump administration functions. But a small group, inevitably, came knocking for the wrong reasons. They thought Corey would take their causes, no matter what they were, directly to President Trump, which he refused to do. And a few of them were just crazy. One guy actually offered him a million dollars if he would get Steve Bannon to pose with him for a photo. Corey told the guy to just hide in the bushes and save his money.

By the spring of 2017, Corey realized that his partner was trying to profit off his name, and he ended the partnership. Unbeknownst to Corey, his partner started doing business overseas and Corey was besieged with individuals and companies in foreign countries wanting him to advocate to the president on their behalf. He refused to do it, even though there was significant money involved. For example, Corey knew of one lobbyist who went out and got a foreign country to pay him millions of dollars up front to lobby the president. This particular person had volunteered on the Trump campaign in California and it's safe to say the president wouldn't know him from a parking meter.

Corey parted ways with the consulting firm in May 2017 and started his own company: Lewandowski Strategic Advisors, LLC.

The press didn't give up on him. That summer, Corey

would grace the cover of the *New York Times Magazine*. "Grace" might not be the right word. They had him on one of those tearaway advertisements you see for dog walkers on telephone poles. The ad read: "I can teach YOU how to influence the president!" The story was the usual lies and misrepresentations, keeping Corey squarely in the media's crosshairs because of his close relationship with President Trump.

Though part of the *Times* story about Corey was pure Fake News, its description of the lobbying industry being rife with dirty money and dubious motivations had some merit. It's also in the lobbying industry where some of Trump's enemies reside.

We don't want you to get the wrong idea: not all lobbyists are bad people. The practice of lobbying is woven into the American political fabric, a convergence of the free market and democracy—a $3 billion a year industry. There have been lobbyists since the 1780s, when New York merchants wined and dined congressmen to sway their votes on a tariff bill. The name comes from the days just after the Civil War. It's said that Ulysses S. Grant would sit in the lobby of a Washington hotel smoking cigars and sipping brandy. While there, he was inundated by "lobbyists" who would ply the president with booze for favors. In the 1970s, K Street became home to Washington's lobbying industry, and it stayed that way through the 1990s, when Grover Norquist and his K Street Project ruled the block. Though the business is still called K Street, most lobbying firms are downtown now, which is all very interesting, but the point is, there are lobbyists who do their jobs inside the appropriate boundaries of ethics and standards.

But there are lobbyists who don't.

Immediately following the election of President Trump, the transition team was inundated with lobbyists who wanted to work in the administration. Many of these individuals are the true swamp creatures of Washington. They use the revolving door in Washington to go in and out of administrations to help their friends. One such person who was never a Trump supporter but found his way into the administration is Mike Catanzaro, a former oil and gas lobbyist. According to the Romney Readiness Project, Catanzaro was slated to be a senior staffer at the Environmental Protection Agency. We all know how that turned out.

Fast-forward four years and, after not supporting candidate Trump, Catanzaro found his way into the White House as Special Assistant to the President for Domestic Energy and Environmental Policy. This gave Mike a huge portfolio, essentially overseeing all energy policy for the country—the problem was it was clear to us and others that Catanzaro didn't support the America First agenda.

Not everyone who is an enemy of President Trump is politically motivated, or rather, has politics as their primary motivation. Many attack or obstruct the administration and president because they are out for themselves.

The federal government of the United States, which was designed as an arm to enforce laws and keep Congress in check, has become a breeding ground for some of the most powerful obstructionist forces in the country. It's where the Deep State resides.

Some of this dark force is made up of individuals like Gary Cohn. According to Bob Woodward's book, Cohn stole documents off the Resolute Desk in the Oval Office that he didn't want the president to see. In one case, the document was the draft of a letter to the president of South Korea that would have reversed an unfair trade agreement. Cohn, who as far as we know didn't receive a single vote in the 2016 presidential election, decided that he didn't want America to withdraw from the treaty. So he took the document so the president wouldn't see it. People like Cohn and Rob Porter, whom we'll talk about in a bit, believe they have the right to change policy by themselves. They think that their opinion matters more than the sixty-million-plus Americans who voted for Donald Trump. Think about that. How narcissistic, how cowardly do you have to be to think you're more important than all those people? One of the greatest parts of our democratic system is that we hold our elected officials accountable for their actions. Yes, Cohn and Porter spilled their guts to Bob Woodward, so perhaps there's a measure of accountability (although they believe they're heroic). What about those times they didn't tell Woodward about? Who gets the blame if their actions cause hardship and harm?

Both Cohn and Porter would later dispute Woodward's reporting, but not in a very convincing way. We hope they were misrepresented. If Woodward got it right, however, they deserve all we've said and more. When the history of this presidency is written, people like Gary will be remember for being disloyal to President Trump.

Along with these individual subversives, there are also unelected officials who litter the federal government and who work in concert, either wittingly or unwittingly, to inhibit policy and sabotage the presidential agenda.

To explain how such a scenario happened, we'll have to take a look back through history. The path from a small, controllable form of government in the United States to the sprawling behemoth we now call "the administrative state" was a long one, and it will take a lot to walk it back. But bear with us; this information will allow you to understand how the embedded enemies of President Trump came about.

It might surprise you to learn, for instance, that the United States of America is not really a democracy—at least not in the literal sense of the word. It's actually a democratic republic. This means that we as citizens don't actually vote very often. Instead, we elect our leaders, and then those leaders cast votes on our behalf. Because of this, voting in these bi-yearly elections is really the only chance we get to participate in our "democracy."

This isn't necessarily a bad thing. If the United States were a true democracy, every citizen in the country— all 360 million or so of us—would be like mini-senators. Every time anyone wanted to pass a law, whether they were a farmer in Iowa or a stock trader in New York City, we would all have to take a vote. If the number of people who wanted something passed was higher than the number of people who didn't, then that thing would pass, no questions asked. Because of logistics and other concerns, this could never work on a federal level in the United States. We don't know about you, but having to consider legislation and vote on things every day wouldn't leave us much time for running campaigns, writing books, or yelling at people on television, which we consider our three callings in life.

All in all, we think the framers of the Constitution did a pretty good job.

But there is one thing they didn't account for—and it's the very thing that is now threatening to choke the life out of this country and strip its citizens of all power and influence in their own government.

Though it's called the Deep State today, it was originally called by many names. Philosophers like Hegel called it the "administrative state," after the do-this, don't-do-that role that it would play in the lives of ordinary citizens. More recent commentators like Michael Lofgren have named it the "Deep State," suggesting it's too far down in the fabric of our country to do anything about, and that most people don't even know it's there. Those people are partially correct.

For a long time, the Deep State consisted of people at large bureaucracies and government agencies that no one ever really thought about—organizations like the EPA and the DOJ. But recently it has ballooned, growing to include additional organizations like the press, the intelligence community, and even the White House and Congress. It has spread like a cancer, and it's become almost impossible to get rid of.

Unlike senators and presidents, the people who work in these organizations are never elected, and they can't be impeached. Only a very small percentage are appointed by presidents. For the most part, they're hired and promoted just like employees at your local bank or shoe store. There's often very little experience required, and these individuals, by and large, are supposed to be "non-political." But look at Andrew McCabe, Peter Strzok, Lisa Page, and so many more "non-politicals" and see the damage they have done to the country. These are the types of individuals who make up the Deep State. They are by no means the only ones; they hide under the cloak of career employee status subverting elected officials' agendas that don't fit their own. They are rooted deep in the government—they only come up from the bottom when necessary—but they have enormous power over the lives of the American people.

Because there's no political litmus test, many of these employees are Democrats. They work hard for liberal presidents like Obama and Bill Clinton, then white-knuckle it through eight years of a Republican, slow-rolling and obstructing their agenda at every turn. This has created a permanent branch of government for one political party—one that never changes, and can't be voted away.

These employees are also promoted largely based on seniority rather than any good work they've done or policies they've helped enact. Government laws—which they created, by the way—make it almost impossible to fire them, and the only people who can fire them are just as reliant on the system as they are. Between the lines of the Constitution, agents of the Deep State have penciled in an infallible system to keep themselves in power forever.

This kind of system—or at least the potential for it— goes all the way back to the early nineteenth century. In those days, the United States was just finding its footing as a country that would someday span an entire continent. To compensate for all that chaos and uncertainty, the government had grown to about ten times what it was at the time it was founded. There were new agencies popping up every year, and more people going into government to oversee them than ever before.

For the first time, the United States government was providing jobs that pretty much anyone could do.

Today, our government is about four times bigger than

it was fifty years ago. It's financed almost totally by debt, and contains more federal agencies with more employees than anyone knows what to do with.

Thanks to this massive structure and the crazy rules that come with each agency, the people who work at the lowest levels of government know how to kill legislation without ever having a public hearing for it. They can stop review processes that need to be done, hold up an amendment on a bill, or simply refuse to comply with orders, sticking the legislation in their desk until someone finally notices. And when someone does, there's no structure in place for punishing or firing that person.

Through their use of the federal rules-making process, Administrative Courts, with their enforcement powers and their knowledge of an arcane system, have made themselves into a secret fourth branch of government, which no citizen of the United States has any power to do anything about. President Donald Trump is taking on this broken system with his strong deregulations approach to government. However, there is still one question that remains: who will win, the Deep State or Donald Trump?

When Donald Trump first began running for president, not many people thought he had sophisticated views on policy or the history of democracy in our country. They were wrong.

Donald Trump has been a student of government and economics for as long as he's been in business for himself. The lessons he's had come from books and also from hard experience and a better intuition with people than we've ever seen. So, when he asks someone to do something for the benefit of the country—especially when it's for people in the country who voted for him, supported him, and are counting on him to preserve their livelihood—he takes it very personally. And he's not going to stand for the fact that the people saying no to him are part of the system that's been choking our country to death.

As far as Trump's enemies go, the big hoaxes like Russian collusion take up all the air and press. But the people who don't get the attention, the swamp creatures who crawl out of K Street and are embedded in the administrative state, attack the administration with a thousand cuts. They do this in complete disregard to the millions of Americans who voted for Donald Trump. They do it only for their own ends. There are far too many people in the deep reaches of the federal government who harbor as deep a hatred of Trump as does anyone from the Clinton/ Obama cabal. The thing is, they get away with it when no one is looking.

President Trump promised the American people he would streamline the government to be more efficient and save the taxpayers' money just as he did in his business. When this commander in chief finds out someone's job is unnecessary, that person is gone. One of the first questions this president asks when presented with a proposal is "How much will it cost?" He thinks of the taxpayers' wallet every moment. We've heard many stories from the highest military officers. One general said that after presenting Trump with a plan of attack in a specific region, the president asked how much each missile costs. The general didn't know, but found it out quickly. We know better than anyone, when the boss asks for a dollar amount, you'd better be accurate and have it within two cents of the dollar—otherwise, prepare to hear about it. As a result of this management style, military efficiency has improved dramatically since President Trump took office, and when missiles are sent overseas the plans are reviewed carefully and selected with excruciating precision. In that respect, Donald Trump is no different from his father, Fred, who would go around and pick up nails from the ground of his construction sites. With Trump, every dollar counts, and every employee needs to perform at peak capacity.

But there are some people in the federal government and other agencies who don't take kindly to cuts. Taking up space and slow-rolling legislation they don't agree with, after all, has made them money for decades and has kept them safely behind their desks for their entire careers. When a president comes into office and says he's going to take away their ability to do that, they get mad. And that's when they assume power to which they have no right.

One of the ways in which the Deep State abuses its power is by hoarding information and keeping it from the public. It's easy to forget, but when a person takes a job with the federal government, he or she is effectively an employee of the American people. That means that every piece of paper or line of text that crosses his or her desk is technically subject to review by the American people. The same goes for meetings this person attends, people they see, and money they spend. At any time, a citizen of the United States can ask to review it.

The process for doing this, however, is not so simple. It was set up by the Freedom of Information Act, which allows citizens to make specific requests for materials that the government is legally obligated to fulfill—or at least respond to with a message saying why that request can't be fulfilled. As you might expect, this system goes awry pretty often, and the scales are tilted toward the people who hold the information in the first place. Still, Dave via Citizens United has gotten a lot of good material by simply filing FOIA requests. They found out, for example, that Hillary Clinton abused her post at the State Department to bolster her crooked foundation. Most of the time, however, the government rejects Dave's requests out of hand, saying they are "overly broad" or "burdensome." When this happens, it needs to be solved by a lawsuit, but that's not something the average citizen can afford.

In the fall of 2017, Dave received a tip saying that Christopher Steele, the author of the infamous fake dossier, had a contact in the State Department under John Kerry that no one knew about. This person was alleged to be former assistant secretary of State for European and Eurasian affairs, Victoria Nuland. Nuland was a Russia expert with decades of government service in the swamp. If it were true, according to this source there would be State Department documents to back it up, and Nuland's role would be subject to a FOIA request. Immediately, on October 20, Dave started checking on the background of the source. When he realized this person was legit, he had someone draft up a FOIA for her records. On October 20, they filed a request, which looked like this:

> In accordance with the Freedom of Information Act, I hereby request all emails sent and received by former Assistant Secretary of State for European and Eurasian Affairs Victoria Nuland for the referenced time period. Furthermore, I request all telephone message slips and/or telephone message logs for

former Assistant Secretary of State for European and Eurasian Affairs Victoria Nuland for the referenced time period. The time period for my request is March 1, 2016 - January 25, 2017.

The State Department's system for filing FOIA requests, at least in the early stages of the process, is pretty simple to use. A request can be filed in a matter of minutes, and upon filing, the department will send an email back confirming receipt of the request.

It's ironic how difficult it can be to actually get anything useful out of the State Department in a timely manner once the Freedom of Information Act request has been filed.

There's a running joke at Citizens United that if you don't sue the State Department in federal court for your requested FOIA records, you might finally get something years and years later, after the topic has been long forgotten.

A few months went by, and the State Department had sent nothing relating to the request. So, continuing a trend that was becoming far too common, Dave filed a lawsuit against the State Department that alleged the following:

When left to their own devices State Department bureaucrats in the past have taken over three years to respond to Citizens United's FOIA requests. Such extensive delays are in clear violation of both the letter and the spirit of FOIA . . .

"Citizens United requests that the Court grant all appropriate relief for the violations of FOIA alleged above, including... [a]n order and judgment

requiring the Defendant to conduct a search for
any and all records responsive to Citizens United's
FOIA request and to demonstrate that it employed
search methods reasonably likely to lead to the discovery of all records responsive to Citizens United's
request . . ."

During the spring of 2018, Dave's legal team was negoti-
ating a production schedule for Nuland's records and
a joint status report needed to be filed with the court.

Dave was optimistic. Asking for one person's emails
over an eleven-month period is not an overly broad request.
Also, from a workload standpoint, the State Department
should have been able to conduct a search like this quickly.

Historically, federal judges have done an excellent job
for the most part of ordering the State Department to turn
over Clinton's records in a timely fashion because it was in
the public's interest. Nothing was different in the Nuland
case; more than sixty million Trump voters were interested.

What came back next was astonishing. The State
Department would be able to fulfill the request, but it would
take somewhere between forty-four and sixty-five years to
do so. Thinking a mistake had been made and the department actually needed forty-five to sixty-five *months*, Dave
asked for the documentation, which confirmed that the
State Department would indeed release the records, but
they would probably do it after he and everyone involved in
the request was long dead. Dave narrowed the search and
the State Department agreed to shave a few years off the
production schedule.

What came next shows how the Deep State really works.
Dave filed another lawsuit for contracts between Christopher

Steele and the State Department. In a delay tactic, the State Department asked Dave to provide the State Department contract numbers—which are not available to the public— in order to complete the search. After a long delay, they finally agreed to search for their own contracts. If that's not the Deep State subverting the will of the people nothing is.

When people have access to the truth, the Deep State can't survive. The best disinfectant is transparency— unelected, unappointed bureaucrats, friends of the Obamas and Clintons have no interest in ever giving up the power they have obtained, and that's why the election of President Trump has upended Washington, D.C.

INTERVIEW
WITH THE PRESIDENT
OF THE UNITED STATES
DONALD J. TRUMP

[Authors' note: This interview was conducted in the Oval Office and lasted about forty-five minutes. Along with White House Press Secretary Sarah Huckabee Sanders and White House Deputy Chief of Staff for Communication Bill Shine, Vice President Mike Pence joined us about halfway through the interview. The interview was edited and condensed for clarity.]

David N. Bossie (DB): This book is about your historic successes, your accomplishments, and the battles you've had to wage on behalf of the American people to do exactly what you promised to do.

Corey R. Lewandowski (CL): The book talks about your battles with the Fake News, the elites on the Hill, people like Bill Kristol and Rick Wilson . . .

President Donald J. Trump (The President): Can you believe this? They take my agenda that I've gotten approved, biggest regulation cuts in history, biggest tax cut in history, ANWR, they've been trying to get it approved for sixty years. More judges than anyone has ever appointed.

*[Authors' Note: ANWR refers to a plot of oil-rich
land in Alaska called the Arctic National Wildlife
Refuge. President Trump took the first steps toward
allowing oil drillers to operate on a 1.6-million-
acre coastal plane in this area.]*

ENEMIES OF YOURS?

DB: Who or what is the biggest enemy of you or your administration?

THE PRESIDENT: The greatest enemy of this country is Fake News. I really mean it. It's hard to believe they get the word out and they stick with it. It is collusion, because they work together. You'll see some things, like a certain phrase will be used, and they'll stick together, and if it doesn't work, they'll go on to the next thing. And they'll all do it in unison. The newest one, that started last week, was "chaos in the White House." It's very dangerous what's going on with the media. Very dangerous. And you've gotta have a lot of different outlets. The other thing that's very dangerous is social media. You look at Google, all of these things that are so far Left-leaning. For instance, if you look under Trump, they show bad stories. They show very few good, and mostly bad.

When I said enemy of the people, I didn't say the media, I said the Fake News. There's a difference. The amazing thing is that you have certain people who are conservative Republicans that if my name weren't Trump, if it were John Smith, they would say I'm the greatest president in history and I blow Ronald Reagan away.

CL: George Will, Bill Kristol, all these guys.

THE PRESIDENT: All these guys that if they looked at my agenda, just with a different name . . . And he got the biggest regulation cuts in history in less than two years, judges, environmental stuff, getting out of the Paris horror show. If you said that conservative president John Smith did that, they would say he's the greatest president. Far greater than Ronald Reagan. A guy like Bill Kristol is a total lightweight. This guy has called me wrong from the beginning. George Will. Total lightweight.

MEDIA COVERAGE

DB: It's not just what they cover, it's what they don't cover.

THE PRESIDENT: They show certain things, it's what they show. It's surprising that I won! You want to know the truth? The system is so badly rigged by the media, including the modern forms of social media, it's almost impossible for me to get a good story out of the *New York Times*. I think that one of the most important things that I've done, especially for the public, is explain that a lot of the news is indeed fake. I look at stories about myself, it might be good or bad. And, I don't mind a bad story as long as it's true. But they'll take a great story and make it bad. Like Kim Jong Un. They couldn't believe when he wanted to meet with me, and then we had a summit. By the time the morning came along, they said "Trump has agreed to meet! This is a tremendous defeat!" They took this unbelievable thing, and they made it into something bad, like I made all these concessions. You know what the only concession I made was? I agreed to meet. That was a big concession. The good news is that for the most part, the public sees through it.

The worst is that it's hard to defend yourself. The advantage of social media is that I can defend myself—I mean social media is skewed to the left—but at least I have my way of getting my message out for instance. They write things about me that are no problem.

MUELLER INVESTIGATION

CL: You saw that James Comey said that he thought the Muller investigation was in the fourth quarter. What do you think he means?

THE PRESIDENT: Did you ever notice that people like you, people who know there was no Russian collusion, nobody calls! They [Mueller's investigators] only call other people and they grab them on things that had nothing to do with our campaign. Every single element of the things that we've seen had nothing to do with our campaign.

You guys know better than anybody that there's no collusion. You know that Bob Woodward's book started about collusion. But he had one problem.

CL: It didn't exist.

DB: His goal was to find it.

THE PRESIDENT: Look, I don't think he's a very good reporter, personally. But I should have talked to him. Nobody told me that he was trying to talk to me.

POLITICIZED INVESTIGATION

DB: So how has the politicized investigation affected your administration?

THE PRESIDENT: I think it makes my base stronger. I would have never said this to you. But I think the level of love now is far greater than when we won. I don't know, what do you think, Mike?

VICE PRESIDENT MIKE PENCE: As strong or stronger.

THE PRESIDENT: In Las Vegas, there are thousands of people trying to get into this one arena. We're not talking about an NCAA championship basketball game, just a guy who goes up and talks and tells the truth.

OBAMA KNOWLEDGE

CL: Do you think, looking back, that Barack Obama knew what [James] Clapper and [John] Brennan and those guys were doing? The insurance policy to spy on the campaign and come after American citizens? Do you think he was aloof or do you think he knew?

THE PRESIDENT: Personally, I think he knew. Yeah. Just remember what they did. Let me put it this way: if the shoe were on the other foot, and the same thing happened to him, it would be treason and they'd be locked up for 100 years.

[On several documents pertaining to the FBI's Crossfire Hurricane investigation, meetings between the FBI and

top members of the Executive Branch are discussed. In
most cases, the names of all individuals who attended
these meetings are listed and unredacted, with the
exception of one. We have several sources who have
informed us that this redacted name is President Barack
Obama. If these sources are correct, it would mean that
Obama had direct knowledge of the surveillance on
Donald Trump.]

JAMES COMEY

CL: Would it have been better to fire Comey on day one?

THE PRESIDENT: Yes. It would have been better to fire him the day after I *won*. Better to fire him on day one to announce please don't be here when I get there. But I almost did that. He was only here for what? Three months? So really, he was there for three and a half months. Really quick. In retrospect, I should have fired him the day after I won and announced please get the hell out. But I really did very early. It's not like I waited a long time. In retrospect, I wish I fired him immediately.

Here's the thing. I didn't do it for popularity. When I fired him, I said "wow." This will be really bipartisan. This will be very popular. Because Chuck Schumer and Nancy Pelosi, saying you gotta fire him. I can't think of one that was positive. Everybody hated him. The Republicans, likewise, hated him. So, when I fired him, I said this is going to be very popular. And the minute I fired him, they started saying wonderful things about him. Because it's a very dishonest system in Washington.

ANDREW MCCABE

CL: There's been a lot of discussion about the leadership of the FBI and its role in both the Hillary Clinton email scandal and phony Russia investigation. After [James] Comey was fired he wrote a book, now Andy McCabe [Andrew McCabe, fired Acting Director of the FBI] has a new book coming out, called *The Threat: How the FBI Protects America in the Age of Terror and Trump*. Where's the accountability? This guy lied three times under oath according to the IG [Inspector General's report].

DB: He's a bad guy.

THE PRESIDENT: He's a bad guy.

You have people within government who are unbelievably bad people. He's somebody, if you look at his texts and you look at what he's done, what he did with Hillary Clinton, where he gave her a pass. You have 30,000 emails that were deleted *after* receiving a subpoena. You know people who deleted emails and they went to jail! Let's see what happens to him. He has the nerve to write a book. I actually hear he's against Comey. That they're fighting.

LISA PAGE AND PETER STRZOK

CL: So, Lisa Page and Peter Strzok. Somehow, the FBI let all this happen?

THE PRESIDENT: And so far, the Justice Department is letting it happen. And I think more than anything else, people are angry at that. They go after people who in some cases have done something wrong and in some cases have not, but nothing on the campaign, by the way! Stuff before the campaign ever took place, etc. But more than anything people are so angry that all of these horrible things took place. You may be surprised. How about that Lisa Page? How about when he goes "Great going with the article"? Then they take the article and go after someone with a badge. Don't forget. We were being watched by these people.

NEW POLICIES AND PROCEDURES

DB: So are you considering any policies and procedures to stop what Page and Strzok did?

THE PRESIDENT: The answer is yes. The American people haven't been fooled. They've been the opposite of fooled. The American people are wide awake. And they're watching. It's being exposed. Some great writers. Gregg Jarrett. Judge Jeanine. You guys. You can go on and on. My friend [Jason] Chaffetz, the Utah congressman.

ANONYMOUS

DB: Now we have to talk about the "anonymous" op-ed in the *New York Times*.

THE PRESIDENT: I don't know. Maybe the *Times* did it. Because of how dishonest they are. We have 3,000 people that fit that description. It's a lot. Senior administration officials, it's at least 1,000. And the way they worded it, we checked. That means it's not someone who would be known. This could mean that it's a person I've never met.

WOODWARD'S BOOK

CL: Sir, so thinking back. Woodward writes this book. People talking to him. That's what the media wants to focus on. They want to focus on the salacious things that people have said. Are those people who say that stuff enemies of what you're trying to accomplish?

THE PRESIDENT: Well, Woodward's book, I should have talked to him. I didn't get the calls. And I should have talked to him. If I had talked to him, maybe it would have been somewhat different. But I didn't read the book. I'm not going to read the book. I like to read things that are pleasant. Actually, some of the things he said, like my stance on the military, which he viewed as "you wanna leave certain countries . . ." a lot of people called and said, "Man, that's great." And he made it seem like it's bad. But I always like to talk to people before they write something. But because of how busy everything is, you can't. But I'll tell you something. Every single person that he wrote about has given massive beautiful letters about, *we never said it*. Whether they did or not, we don't know. But they gave me letters that were very strong. Including General Mattis, General Kelly, Rob Porter.

It's human nature [for people to want to talk to the press]. You have people who have been in the Washington scene forever. I haven't. You heard me, I said I had probably been here seventeen times. Then the eighteenth, I'm riding down Pennsylvania Avenue. I tell that at rallies. I look at my wife, I have two hundred motorcycles in front of me, I have ambulances, I've never seen so many machine guns. I'm riding down Pennsylvania Avenue. I love that story. I say,

"Baby, do you believe I'm president of the United States?" But the problem was that I didn't really know people here. Now I do. I probably know everybody. That's a big point. I came here as a person that was in Washington very few times, less than twenty, and probably never stayed overnight. I didn't know anybody in Washington. I was a New York City person. Then all of a sudden, I'm president. So I didn't have the benefit of knowing. Nobody had the success that I've had in the first two years, and everybody was against Trump. But I'll tell you what happens to people, even people who are on your side. They go through life, nobody ever calls. They work hard, they're wonderful, it happened with you two guys, too. I know you two guys better than you think. And then all of a sudden, you hit the hottest campaign in the history of the United States— you had a lot to do with it, Corey, more than people understand—it's a compliment. We had fun, right?

CL: We had a blast.

THE PRESIDENT: We just blew 'em away. It was over before it started. The escalator ride. How long did it take? I said, "I think I'm gonna do it tomorrow, Corey. Set it up." Turned out to be modest! Time has proven that speech to be very modest.

So all these people [working for the me] are good people, regular people. *This is CNN calling, Fox, New York Times.* They're good people. But they're being inundated with calls from reporters that they've been watching on television for 15 years. This is so and so from ABC, we'd like to have you . . . they get seduced, and they start talking big. I don't say they're bad. They're not! The really good ones don't do that. Or they only talk very positively. Or they become stars. Even the press people become stars. So people who never had a call from a newspaper and frankly, if they were on the Obama team, they still wouldn't have a call. Nobody cared.

Some people that are working for me, they become stars for the first time in their lives. Isn't that an interesting thing? They never get calls. It's not even bad, but bad enough. But many times, they just make it up.

Much of it is made-up sources. There are many times that I read a story, and they don't have sources. They say "sources say" and they make them up.

DOCUMENTS REMOVED FROM THE OVAL OFFICE

CL: What's the real story about the document being removed from your desk by your staff?

THE PRESIDENT: You know what that letter was? I said we're going to terminate the crummy [South Korean trade] deal. So, Lighthizer [Robert, United States Trade Representative], he's great, comes in and says he won't even call us back, sir. I said that's great, tell them they have another two days, and after that I'm going to tax their cars. 25 percent on every car that comes in. So Gary [Cohn] said, "Oh you can't do that!" He's a globalist. And he keeps saying oh you can't. So I called up and I read it to him, I said here's the story: We're going to terminate your deal. It's going to be terminated next week. I'm going to tax every goddamn car you sell. So this guy [Lighthizer] walks into my office, and he says, sir, what happened? South Korea is calling me and begging me to come over and make a deal. They wouldn't even return my call. What happened? That was me! Then I've got to listen to this shit. And if I didn't do that, this country would be in trouble.

MIDTERM ELECTIONS

CL: Do you think the Democrats are going to take back the House and how does that affect your relationships with people on the Hill?

THE PRESIDENT: They [Republicans] should have fought harder for things like the wall. Disappointed me in that. I'm friends with all of them. I do well. But they should have fought harder for the wall and border security. They let me down. And historically, it just doesn't happen. Remember, I'm fighting history here. Except for the fact that I'm fighting history, if you look at the fact that—look, I guess it's three times, and it's always after World War II or 9/11 or something. In other words, I guess people feel that they're happy that they won the presidency and they're complacent. But I have a feeling that we're going to do a lot better than people think. You've seen it. It's incredible. I'm trying to get [Dean] Heller in. He was expected to lose easily and now he's up two points.

HILLARY CLINTON

DB: We didn't even get a chance to talk about Hillary! But she's responsible for the whole fake dossier. She paid for the whole thing.

THE PRESIDENT: Can you imagine she did that and they are looking at this [Fake Russia investigation]?

RUNNING FOR PRESIDENT

DB: So, knowing what you've known today, with the media bias and the Democratic hatred against you so strong, do you regret running for president?

THE PRESIDENT: No, I love it! Look: it's so much different than anybody knows. It's been so successful. Nobody has ever done more than I've done in two years. No president has ever done and—you may look at something to do with war, but basically there was no war in the first two years. The only thing that I have is I have a news media that is totally corrupt. And when I say totally corrupt, I mean 85 percent of it is totally corrupt. You can do something great and they will make it look bad, to a point that you don't even understand why they're doing it. Why do they want to make it look bad? Whether it's fixing the military or cutting regulation. But people have no idea how false and corrupt much of the media is. When you read some of these stories, you pick up the *New York Times*, and they don't call you for sources. They'll say "sources say" and there are no sources. So that would be the one thing that surprised me. The level of corruption and the level of Fake News.

GREATEST ACCOMPLISHMENT

CL: If the American people could only remember you for one thing, what is the single greatest achievement so far of your presidency?

THE PRESIDENT: So, I would say that it would be the economy, and that means a whole lot of things. That takes care of regulation, taxes, everything. So, number one would be the economy and putting people to work. More people are working today than in the history of our country. Millions and millions of people who were never working before. More people working today.

And the other thing would be judges. When I got here, I had 145 judges [vacancies], and Court of Appeals judges. The reason is President Obama, for whatever reason, got tired or bored or something, and when I came here, I had 145 judges! We've gotten 68 approved, and you'll get the exact number but I think it's 68. That's a big deal. When I finish, if I go just by a normal attrition rate, you know, judges retire, they leave office for various reasons including health and age, it's possible that I'll have replaced more than 50 percent of the judiciary. Not including, so far, looks like two Supreme Court judges. He [Brett Kavanaugh] should get approved. It's terrible what they're doing to him. His character, what they're doing.

BEST PART OF YOUR JOB?

CL: What's the best part of your job? You had it all before you came here. What's the best part of being the president?

THE PRESIDENT: Well, we're doing a lot of good things for a lot of people. And I'm enjoying doing it. I'm enjoying doing it. We're doing a lot of good for a lot of people.

DB: Even with all the anger and the resistance?

THE PRESIDENT: It looks like in the real polls that no one comes close to beating us. So far, it's a dream ticket. And people get it. Why are there people standing twenty blocks long to get into an arena, and I won't be there for four hours? People are getting it.

MANAGEMENT STYLE

CL: You ran a business. When you were on the 26th floor, everybody came to you, and you made all the decisions. Everybody came to you and they *Let Trump Be Trump*. That's what I saw from day one. The structure of the White House is very different from what you're used to. How is it different?

THE PRESIDENT: This is probably, maybe it's the right thing, but it's certainly a different atmosphere. I don't know that it's better for me. The other thing might be better for me. More open. More of an open atmosphere. Because some people who wanna get through just don't know how to get through. I like to have people get through. But it's very organized. It's unbelievably non-chaotic.

CL: I think it's the opposite. You like the action. You like to make decisions and—we're saying the structure is very different from the 26th floor.

THE PRESIDENT: I think so. And I could change the structure if I wanted to. It's actually very calm. Now the press likes to create stories. Just last week I was sitting here with some of the biggest executives in the world about economic development coming to the United States. And we go into the other room and the television is on. They have a reporter on from a certain network and he's saying, "Donald Trump is upstairs in the living quarters and he's throwing tantrums and he's throwing fits." And he's outside, and I'm inside, calmly talking to some of the biggest executives. And they say, "Sir, you're not upstairs." They're Fake News. They're liars.

[The president stood and we did too. He came around the Resolute Desk and shook our hands and wished us good luck with the project. We then walked with Sarah Huckabee Sanders and Bill Shine out of the Oval Office, passing the vice president (who had left the interview) who was on the way back in. With that, the president was on his way to the rally in Las Vegas, and we had work to do on the book.]

CHAPTER 13

FAKE NEWS

ON THE NIGHT OF APRIL 28, 2018, we accompanied the president on the smaller Air Force One to a rally at the Total Sports Arena, a venue complete with batting cages and basketball courts in Washington Township, Michigan. The event was a little out of the way. We literally had to drive on a dirt road to get there. When we arrived, however, there were thousands of screaming fans lining the streets and outside in the parking lots and another ten thousand in the arena.

Back in the other Washington, in the ballroom of the Washington Hilton hotel (where President Reagan was shot), there was considerably less applause. It was the night of the annual White House Correspondents' Association Dinner, an event that pretty much everyone in the nation's capital now considers a bore but attends anyway for the free booze and the chance to rub shoulders with celebrity guests.

It's the night when the media and the White House pretend to be buddies and take good-natured shots at each other onstage. If it sounds phony, it is. A rally in a working-class place like Washington Township would perfectly serve as an intentional counterpoint to the elitists having filet mignon back in D.C.

Meanwhile, onstage, the president was in top form. He'd been the first Republican to win Michigan in the general election since George H. W. Bush in 1988, and he showed his appreciation to the crowd—he even called us both up onstage—and the crowd gave it right back to him. The event was wild, joyous.

On the way home on Air Force One, the president invited us to sit with him in his cabin. Lara Trump, the president's daughter-in-law, had come along on the trip, and she was in the cabin, too.

As we sat, the president was flipping channels when he realized that the White House Correspondents' Dinner was still going on. The start time to the dinner had been held back so as not to compete with the president's speech, which was covered by all the cable news channels. On the screen was a so-called comic named Michelle Wolf, whom we had never heard of before. Calling her a comic is a stretch—there was nothing funny about her, and she bombed badly. It would have been one thing if she just wasn't funny, but she was much worse than that. She mistakenly thought the more hateful and caustic she was, the more famous she would become.

Her attempted humor wasn't well received across America or on Air Force One. We sat with the President of the United States and Lara as Wolf tried to be funny. However, all she was was malicious and crass—making jokes about Don Jr., Ivanka, and Eric Trump. Her attack on Sarah Huckabee Sanders was particularly nasty.

We had just left a raucous, uplifting event where thousands of people laughed, cheered, and went home happy, only to witness the mainstream media make a boring spectacle of themselves. It was sad, really.

President Trump has declined invitations to both correspondents' association dinners that have been held since he's taken office. He'd rather be with the real people than the Fake News.

The 2017 version of the dinner was only a little better than 2018. One of the journalists they honored was Bob Woodward. From the dais, Woodward said: "Journalists should not have a dog in the political fight except to find that best obtainable version of the truth." Woodward's made a pretty good living reporting his "version of the truth."

His new book, *Fear: Donald Trump in the White House,* is no different. Only this time, it's not establishment politicians and big-name celebrities he's allowing to rant; it's a group of people who've been slighted in one way or another by the president of the United States and are now trying to make him look bad in public. Woodward picked favorite sources and painted them as heroes, and these sources rambled on for hours, telling fake stories and twisting the truth to suit themselves until they were blue in the face.

Reporters like Woodward once set the standard for journalism, but now he finds himself wanting to make the news instead of reporting the news. People like CNN's White House correspondent Jim Acosta and Don Lemon, host of *CNN Tonight,* are self-important, egomaniac Trump haters who don't care about facts. They care only about their careers. As do most members of the media who sit in the makeup chairs of MSNBC and CNN every day.

Look, we're political operatives and television commentators. It's our job to know the percentages. We know that there's a significant amount of people across America who watch liberal cable news and read the *New York Times* because they're hoping to see President Trump fail and he keeps disappointing them. We know the press trades on the emotions of their audience. The more they stir them up, the more they get them to buy their newspapers, tune in to their channels, or click on their websites. The relationship today the liberal press has with its customers is purely transactional: we'll give you the Fake News about President Trump that you crave, and you buy what we advertise.

The great untold secret about the media relationship with the president is that the press needs Donald Trump as much as they despise him. Without President Trump, the whole business of reporting Fake News collapses.

So it's no wonder the days of unbiased reporting, where a reporter just reported the news and didn't try to make the news, or adjust the news to fit their bias, are long gone. What had once been the venerable Fourth Estate has now become little more than the public relations arm of the Democrat Party, and the very idea of objectivity has disappeared completely. The firewall that once existed between journalists and the people they cover is nonexistent. It's no wonder that the mainstream media exhibits such an obvious liberal bias; none of these reporters ever knows when they might get a promotion and get to work for the next Democrat in the White House.

The Media Research Center recently released a poll revealing that a whopping 90 percent of the major network news stories about President Trump are negative. Ninety percent! No wonder the majority of Americans don't realize the amazing accomplishments this administration makes every day.

The Media Research Center also reports that most of these negative stories aren't even true. One of these fake stories came in the first hours following President Trump's swearing-in, in January 2017. The president was still getting accustomed to the Oval Office when he allowed the press in for his first photo op inside the Oval. Zeke Miller, then a reporter for *Time* magazine, tweeted that "the Winston Churchill bust is back in the office," and that President Trump had removed a bust of Martin Luther King, Jr. from the Oval Office. Twitter was all too happy to take this Fake News and run with it, calling the president a white supremacist and a Nazi before Zeke even had a chance to turn around and look at the rest of the room. Miller would confirm the fact that he rushed to make news, but the damage had been done. The MLK bust was still in the same exact spot it had been when Barack Obama was in office, sitting just below a painting of the Statue of Liberty.

Today people tune in or click on stories like the one about Anthony "the Mooch" Scaramucci, who was accused by CNN of being part of a Russian plot to support candidate Trump. The story was a complete and utter lie. After it was printed, the Mooch managed to get a formal apology from a news station—a rarity during the Trump presidency.

In late November 2017, ABC's investigative chief, Brian Ross, reported that President Trump had ordered General Flynn to contact Russian officials during the campaign.

At the time it was an explosive allegation that sent shudders through the financial markets—the Dow Jones index dropped 350 points. The story was so outrageously false, even the Fake News wouldn't back it up. ABC News suspended Ross immediately and fired him many months later, but the fact that that story led a network news broadcast proves how little the mainstream media cares about honesty.

Another example of Fake News was the story about United Nations ambassador Nikki Haley's curtains. The *New York Times* and just about every other liberal media outlet reported that the Trump State Department spent more than fifty thousand dollars for curtains in the official ambassador's apartment in Manhattan. The purchase was approved during Obama's administration. The *Times* had to run a retraction of the story. The press has had and continues to have only one objective, and that is to harm and eventually take down President Trump.

There has been little to no accountability for any of the journalists who bungle stories. In fact, sometimes they are rewarded for their mistakes—Brian Ross recently was hired as an investigative reporter for another outlet covering Trump.

During election night coverage, Van Jones called Corey a "horrible person" for nothing more than being happy after Trump won. Jones now has his own show on CNN. Nate Silver, the "king of polling" from the website FiveThirtyEight who gave Donald Trump less than a zero percent chance of winning, has written a book and gotten right back to his faulty prognosticating. Paul Krugman of the *New York Times,* who predicted markets would tumble and never recover from a Trump win, still writes his column; Don Lemon and Fareed Zakaria have all yet to express any regret for their biased and derogatory coverage of Donald Trump. And that's only the *Times* and CNN!

Much like the Grand Canyon or the field at Yankee Stadium, this kind of bias is the kind of thing you hear about often but which can't truly be appreciated unless you've seen it with your own two eyes. We've had the rare opportunity of seeing it from the outside and the inside— as both television commentators in front of the camera and as targets of biased, Fake News. We've also worked for the number one target of Fake News, Donald Trump.

In March 2018, the Fake News took its intrusion into Corey's life to the next level. Corey's office is in a town house not too far from the Capitol Building. During business hours, the front door of his office is unlocked. One afternoon in March, a reporter from *New York* magazine named Olivia Nuzzi came to the townhouse hoping to speak to Corey. When no one answered her knocks after ten minutes (because Corey wasn't there), Nuzzi took it upon herself to waltz right in and start snapping photos, which she later posted to Twitter. She knew exactly what she was doing. She'd texted her boyfriend and asked if he thought she was breaking the law. Her boyfriend told her that she "probably" was. A photo album also went missing that day from Corey's lobby—but the MSM had no interest in reporting on her breaking and entering. If a conservative journalist had done the same thing to, say, Obama advisor Valerie Jarrett it would have been front-page news for a week and someone would likely have gotten fired.

Any ideas of decency or boundaries have disappeared in today's journalism. Actually, many in the MSM praised Olivia as just being an aggressive journalist trying to track down a story.

There are some liberals in the press who have the courage of their convictions, misguided reporters who actually believe in what they're saying and writing. But they are joined by the horde of reporters who just want to create news.

As bad as that horde is, there are, if you can believe it, even worse types covering this presidency. This group of turncoat Republicans and former Republicans have flooded our airways with hatred for President Trump. They are so afflicted with Trump Derangement Syndrome that they have flip-flopped on many policy issues and have become the useful idiots of the left to help forward progressive political messaging. These people are true failures in the sense that they have lost control of their emotions and they have switched sides. We can't get away from these obnoxious and annoying squishes who are constantly on cable TV.

One of the most prominent Trump haters is former conservative Bill Kristol, the founder and editor of the *Weekly Standard* who is jealous and angry. He is a clownish political activist who is angry because he opposes President Trump's America First agenda. Kristol is a card-carrying member of the establishment of the Republican Party that has been tossed from power. He recently announced the creation of a so-called War Machine to challenge President Trump for the 2020 Republican nomination.

Actually, whether or not Kristol is a conservative at all is debatable. Back in the 1970s, he supported the patron saint of liberalism, Daniel Patrick Moynihan, and helped him win the Democrat Senate primary in New York in 1976. Kristol thinks of himself as an expert in politics but he's been wrong so much of the time, the *Washington Post* in February 2016 published a whole list of his prominent screwups.

Along with Kristol's *Weekly Standard,* another magazine that had opposed Trump for president is the *National Review.* Founded by William F. Buckley Jr., the *National Review* was once an iconic part of the conservative movement. On February 5, 2016, it published a collection of angry screeds under the title "Conservatives Against Trump." One of the writers was Glenn Beck, the former Fox host who spiraled into obscurity after he left the network. In his remarks, he wrote: "Sure, Trump's potential primary victory would provide Hillary Clinton with the easiest imaginable path to the White House."

The truth was that no other Republican candidates for president in 2016 would have governed in a more conservative manner than President Trump has. Trump passed historic tax cuts, repealed Obamacare's individual mandate, and led massive reductions in burdensome regulations, all leading to a booming economy. The elites over at the *Weekly Standard,* however, were too busy congratulating themselves on their anti-Trump stance to notice the connection candidate Trump had with the workers from middle America. Not many copies of the *Weekly Standard* are lying around iron mines in Minnesota and coal mines in Pennsylvania.

When you transition over to study the bias in the mainstream media, they have become adept at injecting opinion into news and hiring disaffected Republicans to fire away at President Trump. These networks and newspapers hold out squishy Never-Trump writers and talking heads as if they are in the mainstream of the Republican Party. Yet the Republican rank-and-file voters are supporting the president at record levels. Never-Trumpers are the toast of cocktail parties throughout Washington, D.C., with lobbyists, politicians, and fellow swamp-dwelling members of the media. The epitome of the establishment Republican is one who is now on CNN and MSNBC blasting away at the Trump administration.

Another prime example of these turncoat Republicans is Jennifer Rubin, who claims to be a conservative Republican columnist for the *Washington Post*. Rubin is constantly booked on Never-Trump TV, like MSNBC, for a reason. She plays right into the left-wing networks' playbook. She has advocated for harassment of Trump administration officials. Rubin said on Joy Reid's *Morning Joy* show on MSNBC earlier this year that "Sarah Huckabee has no right to live a life of no fuss, no muss, after lying to the press, after inciting against the press. These people should be made uncomfortable, and I think that is a life sentence."

These hateful ideas were spoken on a panel about civility and to the untrained ear this call to arms came from a person who claims to be a conservative.

Then there is George Will. At one point in his career, Will was considered a thought leader for conservatism. He has gone from a respected conservative talking head who was constantly writing or on TV to a guy who abandoned the Republican Party because he dislikes President Trump.

Will urged Republicans to vote for Democrats in the fall of 2018 and made this ridiculous case: "In today's GOP, which is the president's plaything, he is the mainstream. So, to vote against his party's cowering congressional caucuses is to affirm the nation's honor while quarantining him. A Democrat-controlled Congress would be a basket of deplorables, but there would be enough Republicans to gum up the Senate's machinery, keeping the institution as peripheral as it has been under their control and asphyxiating mischief from a Democrat House. And to those who say, 'But the judges, the judges!' the answer is: Article III institutions are not more important than those of Articles I and II combined." Only an aloof individual who thinks he is better than everybody else would try to make the case that putting Democrats in power in Congress will be good for conservative policy objectives.

Had George Will and his Republican anti-Trump allies had their way, Hillary Clinton would have been elected president. The result would have been a Supreme Court handed over to liberal extremists, a stagnant American economy because of overregulation, and higher taxes. Most offensively, Americans would have had to listen to Hillary Clinton on a regular basis making the case that we need to be even more involved in Syria's civil war and even more government intervention in the U.S. economy. Will announced that he was quitting the Republican Party over Mr. Trump's nomination.

Then there's Bret Stephens, the opinion writer for the failing *New York Times*. Like George Will, Stephens also quit the Republican Party. Ideologically fluid, Stephens transitioned from hawkish Republican to gun-control-advocating independent driven by his dislike of Trump's tone and tough campaign rhetoric.

Stephens once wrote a self-absorbed column where he implicitly blamed President Trump for a hateful caller who left nasty messages for him. He used this example of how Trump is inspiring his supporters to commit acts of violence against reporters. He wrote on August 3, 2018, that he expects that reporters will be killed as a consequence of President Trump's rhetoric against the biased press and concluded "when that happens—and journalists are dead because some nut thinks he's doing the president's bidding against the fifth column that is the media, what will Trump's supporters say? No, the president is not coyly urging his supporters to murder reporters, like Henry II trying to rid himself of a turbulent priest. But neither is he the child who played with a loaded gun and knew not what he did." Love the parallel he makes to Henry II to indicate that he is a true intellectual. Stephens' implication that President Trump is like a child with a loaded gun is a great example of his air of superiority.

It is a classic way for Bret Stephens to create an "I told you so" moment if any reporter gets harmed, because we all know Stephens and his band of Never-Trumpers will immediately blame President Trump for a violent act. These same activists completely ignore the rhetoric from the left that has put Trump supporters in harm's way, like Maxine Waters' numerous calls for violence. Jennifer Rubin's plea for harassment of Trump supporters is another example of the double standard. One could make a strong case that if any Trump supporters are harmed by violent political members of the resistance, we can blame the Republican turncoat members of the Never-Trump movement, including Bret Stephens and Jennifer Rubin, for dehumanizing Trump supporters and implying they are a bunch of racist redneck rubes who are not worthy of respect.

Two members of the media who deserve special mention are Steve Schmidt and Nicolle Wallace, who made names for themselves by stabbing the McCain-Palin 2008 Republican ticket in the back. They were the main sources for *Game Change,* Mark Halperin and John Heilemann's 2009 book about Palin's time on the campaign. When the book was turned into an HBO movie, Schmidt and Wallace used their experiences on the McCain campaign to get famous and understood that disloyalty to the Republican Party can make you rich. Liberals will pay top dollar for former Republicans who are willing to trash their former compatriots and friends on television.

Wallace is so committed to bashing Trump that she banned any mention of White House press secretary Sarah Sanders' quotes on her MSNBC program. The worst kind of hypocrite, the former communications employee of President George W. Bush now demonizes a person who works in her old office. She hates Sanders because Wallace desperately wants to be loved by the Trump-hating viewers of the liberal cable network.

Steve Schmidt is no better. In a brazen act of virtue signaling, he dramatically quit the Republican Party and urged its members to vote for Democrats in the fall of 2018. Schmidt tweeted, "Season of renewal in our land is the absolute and utter repudiation of Trump and his vile enablers in the 2018 election by electing Democrat majorities. I do not say this as an advocate of a progressive agenda. I say it as someone who retains belief in DEMOCRACY and decency."

This is the same guy who we can thank for helping to run a presidential campaign in 2008 that got us eight years of President Barack Obama.

And finally, there's Rick Wilson. A onetime Republican strategist who saw his career prospects dwindling once he witnessed Trump's off-the-cuff, energetic strategy for winning elections, Wilson has called President Trump a "tyrant" and "insecure," comparing him to a third-world dictator just because he liked hiring loyal people. A constant presence on CNN and MSNBC, Wilson is a self-aggrandizing loser who should never be hired by a Republican ever again.

Collectively, the names of liberal media and turncoat Republicans above are only a sample of what President Trump faces every day. Make no mistake, the media is part of a coordinated attack against our duly elected president. They are the propaganda machine for Trump's enemies.

Fake News is not just about what is reported but also about what the media chooses not to cover. George Orwell once said, "Omission is the most powerful form of lie." If you only watch CNN, MSNBC, or read the *New York Times*, of course you're going to think ill of Donald Trump because they only speak ill of him. They'll devote little time to, or bury altogether, the stories of his accomplishments. So, for those of you who only get your news from liberal media or turncoat former Republicans, as a public service announcement, here's a sample of what you missed:

As soon as he assumed the office, President Trump immediately went to work to deconstruct the administrative state and empowered the American worker. He began making good on his promise to get rid of two regulations for every one enacted (he actually got rid of over twenty for each one). According to the American Action Fund, he's saved everyday Americans $70 billion in reduced regulatory costs. He also instituted a freeze on hiring of federal employees, which was the second promise he made in his first hundred-day action plan we called the Contract with the American Voter. We announced the plan during the campaign. During the transition, the Obama administration responded to the president's promise by ordering federal agencies like the U.S. Fish & Wildlife Service and the Transportation Security Administration to hire hundreds of new employees. Obama also ordered the agencies to promote as many internal bureaucrats as they could before the Trump administration took over. What he was doing was stacking the decks of these agencies with pro-Obama/Clinton administrators who would go on to obstruct and sabotage the Trump agenda. As we've said, this was especially the case in the Department of Justice, but other agencies, like the Commerce Department, the EPA, and the State Department, were rife with Obama embeds.

Despite the coordinated and constant attacks against him and his agenda, the president has kept marching forward to fulfill his promises to the American people. In those first days and weeks, he took action against the unfair trade deals that had decimated American factories and the American workforce, by withdrawing the United States from the Trans-Pacific Partnership. He reinstated the Mexico City Policy, which ensured that American taxpayer dollars would no longer go to foreign nonprofits that promoted or performed abortions. He signed an executive order that requested the Departments of Justice and Homeland Security to withhold federal funding of sanctuary cities that aid and abet illegal immigrants. Holding America's safety and security as his highest priority, the president ended the "catch-and-release" policy that allowed parole for illegal immigrants caught crossing the border. He green-lit the Dakota and Keystone pipelines.

He began to dismantle Obamacare.

He picked Judge Neil Gorsuch for Anton Scalia's seat on the Supreme Court and nominated Judge Brett Kavanaugh for the highest court.

He's accomplished all of this while the anti-Trump forces both inside and out of the White House engaged in a sustained campaign to bring his presidency down. Their endgame was to nullify the election and the votes of tens of millions of American, but in the meantime they would settle for making the president's job as hard as possible and to thwart his America First agenda.

The Fake News refuses to report the stock market is booming under Trump, or about record-low unemployment numbers. You won't see the stories about the major tax breaks most Americans are receiving under Trump's historic tax cut. You won't hear them talk about the president renegotiating trade deals that drove manufacturing jobs overseas. They won't tell you we're safer and more respected on the world's stage. They don't tell you that the America First agenda is not only working but exceeding even our own expectations. They don't tell you about Neil Gorsuch.

All they tell you about is Robert Mueller and the Russia hoax.

CHAPTER 14

COORDINATED LEAKS

ONLY DAYS AFTER the fake dossier was dropped and the media response was brewing, Peter Strzok texted lover Lisa Page again, wondering how the Crossfire Hurricane team could make the most use of Comey's purposeful leak.

> Strzok: Hey let me know when you can talk[.] We're discussing whether, now that [the dossier story] is out, we use it as a pretext to go interview some people.

One day after he dropped the dossier on the conference table in Trump Tower—three days before CNN would publish a story about it and *BuzzFeed* would publish a thirty-five-page PDF of the fake dossier in full—James Comey sent around an email about his decision to brief President Trump on the material.

"Media like CNN had [the dossier] and were looking for a news hook," he wrote. "I said it was inflammatory stuff that they would get killed for reporting straight up from the source reports." The next day, Andrew McCabe, his deputy, wrote that "the trigger for [CNN publishing the dossier] is they knew the material was discussed in the brief and presented in an attachment."

Everything had gone according to plan.

Reading these emails, which were sent around to FBI leadership on January 7 and 8, 2017, respectively, we can see James Comey beginning to think of an excuse for what he'd done. He admitted that he gave the mainstream media the "news hook" they had been looking for when he included the material in a briefing to President-elect Trump, suggesting that if he hadn't given the dossier credibility by dropping it on the table in front of Trump, the media might have reported it inaccurately. What we know today, however, is that he and Strzok needed to keep public interest in the Crossfire Hurricane investigation alive, and leaking the dossier was the best way they knew how to do that. Without the air of credibility that Comey gave the dossier, the claims would have sounded just as ridiculous to the public as they really were. They would have been reported as rumors, then allowed to float into the air and die as they should have.

But things had become dire at FBI headquarters since the election, and some acted quickly and recklessly. The Trump presidency had pervaded the FBI headquarters like a virus, and the building leadership, including Comey and McCabe, responded accordingly.

Two weeks later, the FBI made contact with Papadopoulos at his mother's house in Chicago, asking him to come in for an interview at one of their Chicago field offices. They told him that they wanted to talk about Sergei Millian, a Russian businessman who was a major source for the fake dossier. Papadopoulos knew Millian and had been approached by him several times during the campaign. According to his account, the two rarely spoke about anything of substance. But the FBI knew that when they brought Papadopoulos in for an interview. The conversation about the Russian businessman, they would later admit in court filings, had only been a "ruse" to get Papadopoulos into a room. What they were really interested in was Russian collusion, and they wanted Papadopoulos to help them prove it.

For the next few hours, the FBI hammered the young man with questions about Russia and the small group of advisors he had been a part of. Papadopoulos answered them to the best of his ability, although he got a few of the details wrong. When they got to the part about how exactly he knew about the release of the DNC emails that had been stolen by the Russians, Papadopoulos got the timing and amount of their communications wrong. Just over a year later, in September 2018, Papadopoulos would be sentenced to fourteen days in prison for lying to the FBI.

The Crossfire Hurricane team remained on the warpath all the way through the inauguration and afterward, as it called in dozens of people for private interviews, many of which were observed or led by Peter Strzok. On January 24, Strzok and another special agent named Joe Pientka interviewed Michael Flynn about conversations he had during the transition with Sergei Kislyak, who was then the Russian ambassador to the United States. They asked Flynn, who had probably had more than a thousand conversations during his time at DIA, to remember specific details about his conversations with the ambassador and when they took place. When Flynn, like Papadopoulos, got some of the details wrong, he was done for. They would indict him for lying to the FBI just before they did the same to Papadopoulos in 2018.

It didn't help that just after the election, Stefan Halper and his fellow spies-turned-academics at the Cambridge Security Initiative made a very public show of resigning from that group, saying that it had been "corrupted by a Russian influence." Halper, who had just failed to root out "collusion" for the FBI on three separate occasions, handled all the front-page interviews about this pronouncement. Soon the stories linking Michael Flynn to Russia had more fuel than ever, as reporters speculated whether or not the woman Flynn had met during his dinner at Cambridge was in fact a Russian spy, as Halper and his colleagues seemed to be implying. In the end, none of it would turn out to be true. The graduate student really was just a researcher doing a project on Russia, and Flynn's interest in her had been purely professional. But by then it was too late. The FBI had caught Flynn in a lie, and public pressure was mounting. After confusing the details again during a conversation with Vice President Mike Pence, he was fired on February 13, 2017.

Incidentally, the judge who would later find Flynn guilty of lying to the FBI was none other than Rudy Contreras, the judge Strzok and Page had been texting about in July 2016, when they were hoping he would look favorably on their second attempt at a FISA warrant. Contreras had left the Foreign Intelligence Surveillance Court by the time he tried Flynn but never disclosed that he was a personal friend of Peter Strzok—not even when the case went to trial. This calls into question a potential violation of ethics and norms within the Justice Department.

But the media campaign didn't stop with Papadopoulos or Flynn. In April 2017, Strzok and the Crossfire Hurricane team, having found nothing on the phones or emails of Carter Page, decided to conduct a media smear campaign instead. As with all things in his life, Strzok texted Page about the whole thing. On April 10: "I had literally just gone to find this phone to tell you I want to talk to you about media leak strategy with DOJ before you go."

The next day, the *Washington Post* published a story about the FBI's surveillance on Carter Page. Once again, the information wasn't good enough, so Strzok and the FBI relied on mere insinuation to make their case. If they couldn't find any evidence that Carter Page was in contact with the Russians, they could at least put the suggestion into the heads of the public, giving the Russia investigation all the fuel it needed. Shortly afterward, Strzok and Lisa Page shared more articles, noting which ones were "better than the others" and how they came across in each one. Repeatedly, Strzok referred to Carter Page as the "namesake" of Lisa Page (no relation). But the smear campaign didn't work. Unlike Papadopoulos and Flynn, Carter Page had his story straight when the FBI came knocking, and he was never indicted for a crime.

Thus, the FBI investigation into Donald Trump went into the spring of 2017 without any evidence that any member of the Trump campaign had any contact with Russia. Strzok had failed to, as he promised his lover, "protect the country" from his enemy . . . Donald J. Trump.

* * *

James Comey had just as much trouble adjusting to the reality of the Trump presidency. On several occasions, he had private meetings with the president, during which Donald Trump asked him for loyalty—which, as anyone who's ever spent a few minutes with the boss knows, is really just a throwaway line that he'll give you before you enter into some venture together; he's not asking you to treat him any differently than anyone else. But Comey, being the grandstanding, sanctimonious Boy Scout that he is, decided that President Trump's request constituted a national emergency, and started making notes of every meeting he had with the boss. By their nature, these notes were classified. They contained material that wasn't fit to be shared with the media or the public. Officially, two of the memos were classified as "confidential," while two were classified as "secret." From January to March 2017, Comey turned these notes into classified memos, which he sent around to his friends at the FBI, including Andrew McCabe, whom he trusted more than anyone. If that were all he'd done, there would be nothing wrong with it.

But Comey took things one step further when he leaked several of those memos to his friend Daniel Richman, a professor at Columbia Law School who knew people in the media. Over the next months, Comey would work with Richman to ensure two things: that Attorney General Jeff Sessions recused himself from the Russia probe, thereby clearing the way for Rod Rosenstein to make all decisions regarding the matter; and that if he were fired, a special counsel would be appointed.

On March 2, Carol Lee and a few other reporters at the *Wall Street Journal* wrote that investigators had looked into some contacts with Russia that Jeff Sessions had during the transition—things he had lied about under oath. The story was sourced to "people familiar with the matter." That same day, Jeff Sessions recused himself.

Then, in April, Comey leaked more memos that contained information about his meetings with President Trump, all of which were written in language that made the president look as bad as possible. It was the technique he had used with Hillary Clinton's email investigation in reverse, in which Comey took something that was not a crime and used his lawyerly cunning to make it sound like one. The stories contained within the memos, which were soon printed in the *New York Times*, all but ensured that a special counsel would be appointed. It no longer mattered whether Comey and Peter Strzok were fired from the FBI; the investigation into Donald Trump would continue.

On May 9, Donald Trump fired James Comey for being an ineffective director of the FBI. Peter Strzok and Lisa Page were distraught.

"Having a tough time processing tonight, Lis.," Strzok wrote. Lisa Page responded right away.

"I feel that same loss. I want to see what the FBI could become under him! His vision of greatness for our strong but flawed organization. I'm angry. Angry and mourning."

That same day, Strzok texted the following: "We need to open the case we've been waiting on now while Andy is acting."

CHAPTER 15

MUELLER

DEPUTY ATTORNEY GENERAL Rod Rosenstein's appointment of Robert "Bob" Mueller as special counsel was controversial from the start. The public has continuously questioned the need for this appointment as well as the way he has conducted his investigation.

America is headed toward a constitutional crisis. Whether it's a subpoena to the president requiring his testimony or a scathing report to the DOJ and Congress that begins impeachment proceedings, the American people know that this whole witch-hunt investigation is a hoax.

We're not lawyers. But if you ask us, we don't think that President Trump should ever sit down with Mueller, and we'll tell you why. The kind of interview Mueller wants to conduct is essentially a trap by definition—and you don't have to be a lawyer to know that. It's common sense. You have a situation in which one side has a small army of lawyers who almost literally spend every hour of the day devising questions to trip up their subject. On the other side of the table, there's the president of the United States, who just might have a couple of other things going on that take up his time besides preparing for questions about a fake dossier.

Still, we believe President Trump would take his chances with Mueller in a heartbeat—because he has nothing to hide.

As someone who's been part of organizing this sort of thing before, Dave knows all too well how easy it is to tie a subject up or walk them straight into a so-called perjury trap. He knows how lawyers plant a question in the beginning of the interview and then introduce a slight variation ninety minutes later, hoping the subject of the interview will lie by accident and fall into the trap. Dave knows lawyers who know how to get so specific with the facts that no human could possibly recall them all correctly. It's as simple as knowing the answers you want before you ask the questions.

Perjury is a serious crime, and it's also one of the easiest to commit by accident—or to make someone commit against his or her will. No one knows this better than General Michael Flynn.

It was only two days after the inauguration when the FBI came to General Flynn asking if he had, in fact, made a phone call to Sergei Kislyak, the Russian ambassador to the United States, over the expulsion of thirty-five Russian diplomats from the United States on December 29, and whether the content of that call had included possible relief from Russian sanctions. One of the agents who interviewed Flynn was Peter Strzok, the disgraced chief of the FBI's counterespionage section. Flynn also talked that day to the

FBI without a lawyer present. When Flynn said no to one of those questions, for whatever reason, he had committed perjury. When he subsequently lied to Vice President Mike Pence, it was enough to force Flynn out of the administration just a few weeks into his tenure.

The FBI had come at Flynn hard—trying to get him to say something that wasn't truthful. They asked him questions about obscure things he couldn't possibly remember correctly, then used the inaccurate answers to intimidate him, and to give the false collusion narrative the kind of plausibility it never should have had with the public or the media. And it didn't stop there. All throughout January, James Comey and his band of anti-Trump soldiers at the FBI continued tapping the phones of many members of the Trump administration and collecting intelligence on all their movements and meetings. They were building a case against American citizens as if they were members of a terrorist cell operating in the United States.

After witnessing Comey's indecision and mismanagement of the Hillary Clinton email investigation, candidate and President-elect Trump was hearing from the media and Democrats that Comey ought to be fired. By the time President Trump made the decision to fire Comey, the FBI director had committed enough offenses to potentially be criminally charged. He had been willfully insubordinate, refusing to give President Trump information he demanded. He had leaked classified documents and notes of their conversations, hoping to sway public opinion and force the recusal of Attorney General Jeff Sessions. This would allow Deputy Attorney General Rod Rosenstein to appoint a special counsel. And worst of all, as we've said: James Comey abused his power as the head of the FBI to conduct surveillance on people he had a bias against, misleading the Foreign Intelligence Surveillance Courts of the United States into giving him a warrant to do so.

To do that, he and the rest of the intelligence community—including John Brennan, Sally Yates, Bruce Ohr, and James Clapper—had presented a false, unverified dossier as truth, failing to mention that it had been compiled by a foreign agent who had as much hostility toward Donald Trump as they did. In simpler language, Comey had a false sense that he was better than everyone and he hated the way Mr. Trump went about his business.

Lavrentiy Beria, the head of Joseph Stalin's secret police, once said, "Show me the man, and I'll show you the crime."

The American people have now learned that there are individuals inside the FBI who live by those words. Even Bill Clinton, a man who is about as slippery as you can get under questioning, fell into a perjury trap.

The independent counsel, Kenneth Starr, led the investigation into the Clintons for the Whitewater scandal, which was a series of real crimes with real victims. Anyone but the Clintons would have done serious time for those activities. So, when Attorney General Janet Reno allowed Starr to broaden the scope of his investigation, he went for Clinton's apparent perjury regarding sex with women. In his back pocket, Starr knew about Clinton's affair with Monica Lewinsky. But the deposition in which Clinton lied was part of the Paula Jones lawsuit, in which she was suing Clinton for sexual harassment when she worked in Arkansas state government. Jones' lawyer set the trap by asking Clinton if he'd had a sexual relationship with

Monica Lewinsky, and the then president of the United States walked right into it.

"No," he said.

Starr's team used the same strategy with Clinton that the FBI would later use with Mike Flynn, asking him questions that they knew full well might lead him to give a wrong answer to save himself from embarrassment.

The same was true in the case of Scooter Libby, the former chief of staff to Vice President Dick Cheney, who was tried for leaking information related to the Iraq War in 2007 but eventually was convicted of only two unrelated offenses by a special counsel. The story of Libby's supposed crimes is far too complex to go over here, but it's enough to say that he was accused of leaking the name of a CIA operative to Judith Miller, a reporter at the *New York Times*. When it came out that Libby may have been responsible for this, the acting attorney general at the time—none other than James Comey, who was filling in for John Ashcroft, who was in the hospital—appointed a special counsel to investigate the matter.

The special counsel's name was Patrick Fitzgerald, and he was a Beltway lawyer with deep ties to the liberal establishment and the intelligence community. He was also the godfather of one of James Comey's children. Just like today, Fitzgerald, under the close watch of Comey, did everything he could to force a conviction in the case. He tried to pin every crime in the book on Libby but found that nothing would stick. Eventually he made the man sit for an interview, doing absolutely everything he could to make him contradict himself. When that didn't work, he got Miller, the *Times* reporter to whom Libby had supposedly leaked the information, and sat her down for an interview as well.

By the end of that two-hour session, Fitzgerald had gotten all the "answers" he wanted, using the special counsel playbook to force the outcome he'd been hoping for from the beginning. The abuse of power by the special counsel sent Miller to prison for twelve weeks for refusing to falsely testify against Scooter Libby.

As Miller would later write in her memoir, *A Reporter's Life*, Fitzgerald "manipulated her memory" and "withheld critical information," steering her in the wrong direction as she prepared to testify. When the grueling interviews were over and the verdicts were in, Libby had been found guilty of perjury and obstruction.

For these reasons and more, President Donald Trump pardoned Scooter Libby in April 2018, having seen firsthand what kind of abuse a special counsel can inflict on an innocent man. Judith Miller herself praised the president for doing so, writing in an op-ed that she and Libby had been treated very unfairly by the special counsel.

We have no doubt that Mueller is a skilled enough lawyer to "get a grand jury to indict a ham sandwich," as the saying goes. We also know that he owes a certain debt to James Comey, a man to whom Mueller is very close, and he undoubtedly feels that the president has treated his friend unfairly. Still, we don't know whether Mueller, like James Comey, has a hatred for Donald Trump. He's very tight-lipped that way. The journalist Steven Brill put it best when he told *Politico* that asking Bob Mueller to leak information would be "like asking him to watch a porn movie with you."

Evidence shows that Mueller is highly motivated to repay the president for firing his friend Comey and is willing to use the subpoena power of the special counsel to require the president to testify under oath. This will lead America needlessly to a constitutional crisis, potentially forcing this issue all the way to the United States Supreme Court.

On May 16, 2017, only a few hours before Bob Mueller would start looking for secret payments and dark connections between the Trump campaign and the Kremlin, he was sitting across from President Trump for a job interview.

The position of director of the FBI had been vacant for a little over a week; however, rumors that President Trump had fired Comey to "obstruct justice" were already swirling by the Fake News divisions at the networks and the hyperpartisans on Capitol Hill. These same swamp creatures began a narrative that by firing Comey, President Trump had committed a crime—ridiculous!!

In reality, President Trump knew that the investigation wouldn't stop just because he replaced the FBI director. It has now been widely written why the president fired Comey.

Comey claimed he wanted to blend in with the curtains when Trump was in the room, hiding so he wouldn't have to talk to him. We would find out later that Comey was telling friends and coworkers that he viewed the small circle of Trump's advisors at the time—meaning the vice president, Reince Priebus, Steve Bannon, and Jared Kushner— as being like the crime families he'd prosecuted in the 1980s and 1990s. He would later write in his memoir that he thought the conference room in which Trump and a few others had met with him in January was like "a New York mafia social club," and that the newly elected president had been trying to make him into an *amica nostra*, an old mob term meaning "friend of ours," or someone who could be trusted.

James Comey has a vivid and active imagination.

It was clear by May 9 that Comey had come to believe that he was the star of the show, and that the show had suddenly become a made-for-television movie. We think any president presented with Comey's actions before and after the election would have fired him. Period.

Comey's replacement needed to be the antidote to all that—someone who could put the job before himself or his politics. By most accounts, there were only a few people who would qualify for the job and Bob Mueller was one of them. Mueller served as director of the FBI for a longer period than any man other than J. Edgar Hoover himself— he clearly knew the terrain better than anyone. There's no doubt that he also built a reputation for being extremely nonpartisan and pragmatic. But he also began as director during the least partisan time America has experienced since World War II. He began as FBI director just a few days before the attacks of September 11, 2001.

The period of American history after 9/11, however, saw many of the most important fights over civil rights and surveillance—both of which would become very important during the Trump campaign—take place, and Mueller was an integral part of them. He also grew very close during this period to Comey, who was then the deputy attorney general under Attorney General John Ashcroft.

Mueller's biographer Garrett Graff once remarked that in the years after 9/11, Mueller and Comey "probably spent more time together than they did with their wives."

This was odd, considering their jobs. Traditionally the deputy attorney general, who is the FBI director's supervisor, doesn't spend much time with the director beyond meetings here and there. But for some reason Comey and Mueller developed a remarkable relationship, which is kind of hard to define unless you understand the history.

This friendship was never more evident than in March 2004, when Comey found out that the Bush administration was about to reinstate an NSA surveillance program it had come up with just after 9/11, and that some elements of the program were arguably unconstitutional. Ironically, the parts that Comey had trouble with were the ones that involved spying on American citizens—something he would later change his tune on once the right enemy came along. Apparently, based on his actions, he is more than willing to get sanctimonious about protecting the rights of suspected terrorists, as opposed to a straight-talking billionaire businessman. The problem with reauthorizing the program, in Comey's view, was that his boss, Attorney General John Ashcroft, didn't want to reauthorize the program, but couldn't say so because he was in intensive care with severe pancreatitis.

When Comey was driving home on March 12, he got word that George W. Bush's chief of staff, Andy Card, and White House counsel Alberto Gonzales were about to go to Ashcroft's hospital room and have him sign the order that would reauthorize the NSA spying program. Comey saw it as his duty to intervene. He had his driver switch on the flashing lights and speed toward Ashcroft's hospital room, where he lay gravely ill with his wife by his side. According to Comey's testimony, it was Ashcroft's wife who called him and gave him the news. Apparently, on the way to the hospital Comey realized that his actions might come off as grandstanding. He had a reputation for pulling stunts like this in the past—bringing charges against that notorious crime boss, Martha Stewart, for instance—and it was getting harder and harder to believe that he was doing it for anything other than attention.

So he called Bob Mueller, a man who was, as he would later testify, "unimpeachable." If Mueller threatened to resign over the reauthorization of the NSA program, Comey knew, the Bush administration would have no choice but to back down. Within the hour, the two men had entered the hospital and were heading directly to Ashcroft's room. Comey supposedly told Mueller that he should prepare to resist the Secret Service if they tried to remove him from the room. Mueller agreed. When Andy Card and the rest of the Bush entourage arrived, the scene came to a climax, which is really much better if we let Comey tell it himself. Under oath, this is exactly what Jim Comey said about that day:

> Attorney General Ashcroft then stunned me. He lifted his head off the pillow, and in very strong terms, expressed his view of the matter, rich in both substance and fact. Then laid his head back down on the pillow, seemed spent. And said, "That doesn't matter, because I'm not the attorney general. There's the attorney general." And he pointed to me, and I was just to his left. The two men did not acknowledge me. They turned and walked from the room.

Maybe it did happen like that. Maybe people do talk like that in the movies, and maybe Comey has the "contemporaneous notes" to prove it.

Ultimately, the program did end up being reauthorized. The Justice Department rewrote key portions of the program, called Stellar Wind, so that it would be more in line with constitutional protections—or at least less obvious when it strayed from the letter of the law. What they came up with was a framework for spying on U.S. citizens that adhered more closely to the civil rights laws on the books and required almost no warrants for doing so. The set of four programs, each of which remains partially classified and has its own code name, covered four different areas of data collection, and each was approved by the same secret courts that would later give Comey and his FBI the authority to spy on members of the Trump campaign.

There's still no telling what kind of activity the NSA may have conducted under the radar using its massive data centers in Utah, or how many of the technological intelligence-gathering methods outlined in Stellar Wind were involved in the Obama administration's spying on Donald Trump. If the past is any indication, we won't know for decades, when the proper records become declassified. Of course, it's possible that we'll never find out.

Comey and Mueller stayed close over the years. When Mueller finally agreed to step down from his post after twelve years on the job—he'd been appointed by George W. Bush and granted an extra two years by Barack Obama, who agreed to forgo the typical ten-year term limit—James Comey took over. In that time, the FBI grew more political and partisan than it had ever been before, and the abuse of the FISA courts became rampant.

Bob Mueller went back to work at Wilmer Hale, the law firm in Boston where he was made a partner in 2014. There he handled many high-profile cases, including one for the National Football League that came up when Baltimore Ravens running back Ray Rice was caught on video knocking out his wife in an elevator. In his report, Mueller, working for NFL commissioner Roger Goodell's office, even though evidence in the case pointed to the league's culpability, dismissed any wrongdoing. Other than that, he kept his usual low profile and didn't make many headlines. Mueller is the complete antithesis of Comey—one is a worker not looking for headlines and the other is a self-aggrandizing showboat who wants to decide on behalf of the American people what is legal and what isn't.

When it came time to find a new director for the FBI, Muller interviewed with President Trump. We still don't know what the two men talked about when they were in that room together, but we can probably assume it was typical of the questions the president was asking all of the potential candidates who were interviewing for the FBI director position. Just as it had been during the debacle at Ashcroft's hospital room, Comey's first phone call after he was fired may have been to Robert Mueller.

Unfortunately, the content of Mueller's interview for FBI director doesn't really matter, because the very next morning, Deputy Attorney General Rod Rosenstein announced that Mueller would be the special counsel in charge of investigating "any links and/or coordination between the Russian government and individuals associated with the campaign of President Donald Trump." The letter that appointed Mueller also noted that he had the authority to investigate "any matters that arose or may arise directly from the investigation; and…any other matters within the scope of 28 C.F.R. § 600.4(a)."

You can read those last two lines as meaning "anything else you want if you can't make this Russia stuff stick." That last citation is the section of the Code of Federal Regulations that set up the special counsel, and it gives him the authority to do pretty much whatever he wants. What's odd about Mueller's appointment is that Rosenstein didn't inform his superior, Attorney General Jeff Sessions, prior to making the decision. Sessions had recused himself from the fake Russia hoax investigation in March, after he revealed that he, too, had spoken with the Russian ambassador to the United States on a couple of occasions, and Comey leaked his classified memos to get Jeff Sessions to recuse himself.

When Mueller was announced as special counsel we were as shocked as anyone because there was zero evidence that breached the threshold requiring the need for a special counsel. However, of all the people who could have been appointed, Mueller seemed like the one who was most likely to do a thorough job, and to conduct the investigation fairly and without bias. We hadn't yet thought about his deep, incestuous ties to James Comey, or the inherent bias that Comey's firing would create on Mueller's team.

Ultimately, his investigation would be anything but fair.

Whether Mueller holds a grudge toward Donald Trump or not is still an open question. However, when you look at the team he assembled, it's hard not to believe he's at least biased against him. According to multiple news organizations, not a single investigator working for the special counsel is Republican. Twelve of them donated to Hillary Clinton's campaign, with two of them giving the maximum allowed by law.

For his right-hand man, Mueller hired Andrew Weissmann, a lawyer who attended Clinton's election night party. It has also been reported that Weissmann was one of the DOJ officials who was kept apprised of Christopher Steele's phony dossier by Bruce Ohr. Then, to go over some of the early witnesses and fact patterns, Mueller brought on Peter Strzok, the man who had been obsessed with Russia from the very beginning, even refusing to investigate Hillary Clinton's emails in favor of looking into the Trump campaign. It was the assignment Strzok had been dreaming about, and he hit the ground running. A few months in, Mueller also hired Lisa Page, the FBI lawyer with whom Strzok was having a lurid affair, to look over some of the financial aspects of the investigation.

Those two alone compromised the investigation. Their outright bias against Donald Trump and for Hillary Clinton—which would be revealed a few months later, in the infamous IG report—made them unable to fairly investigate Donald Trump. Anything they touched, which, as we understand it, was just about everything, including each other, should be invalidated.

CHAPTER 16

IG REPORT

BY THE TIME the long-awaited Department of Justice inspector general report was released to the public, Peter Strzok had taken charge of the Russia investigation. Other than Mueller himself, there was no one who had more control over what the team looked into or how they conducted themselves. As we said before, it was the assignment Strzok and his paramour, Lisa Page, had been waiting for—one that let them use the full force of the Federal Bureau of Investigation to take down Donald Trump and disqualify the votes of tens of millions of people.

This made what the report found all the more damning. The two had coordinated their efforts to defeat Donald Trump, while absolving Hillary Clinton, long before the man was even inaugurated. In fact, the groundwork for the Russia investigation was in place while the campaign was still going on, and the people who would become Mueller's attack dogs were making plans to nullify the election if he ever won.

On the eve of the IG report being released, we had hoped that it would bring to an end the fake Russia hoax forever.

What happened was a very different story.

For those of you who might not know, the Justice Department's Office of the Inspector General is supposed to act as a kind of independent regulatory division of the agency. The OIG conducts investigations of alleged wrong-doing of DOJ employees, programs, or investigations. If a DOJ employee, say an FBI agent, is thought to have committed a crime, it's the OIG who's charged with investigating them, delivering a report, and advising the agency on how they should be punished. If officials in the Justice Department—and, by extension, the FBI—are cops, then the IG acts as the internal affairs bureau.

At the time of the 2016 election, the inspector general was Michael E. Horowitz, who had been in the role since 2012. Horowitz had worked for a long time in the Justice Department. He was an assistant U.S. attorney for the Southern District of New York for eight years where, from 1991 to 1993, he worked with James Comey (just before Comey worked with Dave on the Whitewater committee). They worked on the same criminal cases together, mostly ones to do with the mafia and organized crime. Barack Obama nominated Horowitz for the DOJ IG position. His wife once worked as a field producer for CNN, and had donated to Barack Obama's 2008 presidential campaign, according to federal records. If our timing is correct, Horowitz was Bruce Ohr's boss in the Criminal Division of the DOJ.

The most important aspect of an inspector general's job is impartiality. Even the appearance of bias corrupts a report. From the start, it seemed Horowitz was off on the wrong foot.

Once he became inspector general, Horowitz crossed paths with Comey again, when he investigated the conduct of the FBI director's deputy, Andrew McCabe, in April 2018. A few chapters back, we told you that Dave wasn't surprised when he found out why McCabe might not have wanted to investigate the new batch of Hillary's emails found on Weiner's laptop. Here's why:

As we've mentioned, Hillary Clinton's email scandal first became public in 2015, when the *New York Times* revealed she had set up a private server in her home that she used for official business. Once that information was out there, it was all but inevitable that the FBI—led by James Comey with Andrew McCabe as his deputy—would have to investigate, even if the "investigation" turned out to be a ruse.

We don't think it's a stretch to say that the last person in the world McCabe wanted to investigate was Hillary Clinton. At the time, his wife, Jill McCabe, was about to run for the state senate in Virginia and received $675,000 for her campaign from political action groups aligned with the Virginia governor and Clinton confidant Terry McAuliffe. It's not hard to tie McAuliffe to dark money funneled to the Clinton Foundation, Clinton campaigns, and the Clinton library. He's a full-service guy; he even arranged for the loan the Clintons took on their house in Chappaqua, New York.

Less than a week after Hillary's email scandal blew up in the media, Jill McCabe met with McAuliffe. A few days later, she announced her candidacy. You must question why McAuliffe was so eager to back her. Did he know that her husband was part of the investigation into his friend who was about to announce her run for president? A lot rode on the Virginia election—Republicans held a razor-thin edge in the Virginia Senate. Jill McCabe had never run for political office. Her primary opponent (who dropped out after McAuliffe met with the McCabes) was a well-known Democrat activist, a retired army colonel, and respected local attorney, according to a popular Virginia Democrat political blog. He had been recruited to run by a local Democrat Party boss.

The whole thing stank to high heaven. Even Strzok and Page have a cameo in the story. Strzok would later blame Jill McCabe's loss on the local "hillbillys" in the district in a text to his girlfriend.

McAuliffe's unusual "gift" to Jill McCabe would become public days before the 2016 presidential election when the *Wall Street Journal* published the story. Only after the story ran would her husband completely recuse himself from the Clinton email investigation, and he did so reluctantly. Meanwhile, the *Journal* was preparing to run a story about McCabe and the FBI slow-walking a different Clinton investigation, this one into the Clinton Foundation. McCabe knew the Clinton Foundation story would blow up his career and paint him for what he was—a stooge for the Clintons. He devised a plan, one that would ultimately get him fired. He had the FBI public affairs officer, and his special counsel, one Lisa Page, leak to the *Wall Street Journal* that not only was he not slow-walking the investigation, but that he was practically the only one in the whole DOJ who wanted it to happen. A true American hero.

On the day Andy McCabe assumed the position as

acting director of the FBI, the inspector general sent investigators to question McCabe about the leaks under oath.
As a reminder, lying to the IG investigators is punishable
with up to five years in prison and a $250,000 fine for each
instance. Andy lied three times that day. Later, Horowitz
filed a report to Congress detailing the leaking McCabe
had done and enumerating the multiple lies he had told to
cover it up—ultimately, the report recommended a criminal referral for Andy McCabe. Taking that information into
consideration, Attorney General Jeff Sessions fired Andrew
McCabe twenty-six hours before he was set to retire from
the FBI. Sessions concluded that anyone who leaks information and lied to the IG on multiple occasions under oath
shouldn't be working for the FBI.

We took Horowitz's report on McCabe as a good sign.
The system worked like it was supposed to: the Inspector
General sends investigators, they find wrongdoing, they file
a report, and then the attorney general acts on that report.
The whole thing was over relatively quickly. Back in the
White House, Donald Trump was very happy with how it
had gone. He tweeted:

> Andrew McCabe FIRED, a great day for the hard
> working men and women of the FBI—A great day
> for Democracy. Sanctimonious James Comey was
> his boss and made McCabe look like a choirboy. He
> knew all about the lies and corruption going on at
> the highest levels of the FBI!

With justice served on Andrew McCabe, we couldn't
wait for what the IG would deliver next.

* * *

Officially called "A Review of Various Actions by the Federal Bureau of Investigation and Department of Justice in Advance of the 2016 Election," the OIG report on the Hillary Clinton email case would look into the conduct of the FBI on a large scale and reveal the extent to which the bureau had favored Clinton and attacked Trump. Everyone in government seemed to know that the FBI had vastly abused its power, and that James Comey had acted unethically all throughout the year, so Congress requested the IG to investigate his conduct. The report was going to include notes on Peter Strzok, Lisa Page, Comey, Clapper, and Brennan, and the rest of Trump's enemies who had been working against the president since day one.

By early June, however, it was clear that Michael Horowitz was being methodical in his investigation. He had told Congress in November 2017, when the investigation began, that he would try to deliver a report in early spring. The longer we waited, the more frustrating it became. We were worried about Horowitz's impartiality. On June 5, the president tweeted:

What is taking so long with the Inspector General's Report on Crooked Hillary and Slippery James Comey. Numerous delays. Hope Report is not being changed and made weaker! There are so many horrible things to tell, the public has the right to know. Transparency!

We had hoped the report would provide us the vindication we'd been looking for since Comey announced Hillary Clinton had "committed no crimes" with regard to her handling of classified information. When it finally came out, Steve Bannon received it with glee, emailing copies and notes about the document to all his friends from the White House. Dave blew through the thing like a paperback thriller at the beach. After all, it promised to be the inevitable indictment of Clinton, Comey, and the rest of Trump's enemies.

The report was more than five hundred pages. Front and center Horowitz placed all the things that were less devastating to Comey and the intelligence community. He hid the good stuff deep in the report.

If you didn't read the fine print, you would have missed the most important parts. The inspector general found that James Comey had absolutely acted improperly when he decided not to charge Clinton, abused his authority, and willfully concealed information from the Department of Justice. Most people call that lying.

The report stated that Andrew McCabe had crossed several lines in his involvement in the Clinton investigation and should have recused himself right away because of the conflict of interest (which is a nice way of putting it) with his wife's campaign.

The report also took aim at Bill Clinton and Loretta Lynch's infamous meeting on the tarmac, saying that it never should have happened, and that it most likely influenced the decision that the FBI made.

The report chastised the FBI for waiting until late October before they got a search warrant for Anthony Weiner's laptop; it said the FBI was "inconsistent with typical investigative strategy and gave rise to accusations of bias and preferential treatment," for letting Hillary's attorneys, Cheryl Mills and Heather Samuelson, come to Clinton's FBI interview. Mills and Samuelson could have been witnesses to her crimes; however, they were given immunity.

Finally, the report put disgraced FBI agent Peter Strzok and former FBI lawyer Lisa Page's anti-Trump furor on display with numerous examples of the texts they sent each other, including the most inflammatory when Strzok assured Page that they had an "insurance policy" against a Trump victory.

As bad as the insurance policy text made Strzok and Page look, it was a prelude to the main event—the finding of the IG report that even Peter Strzok's most strident defenders couldn't seem to explain away. It was a chain of text messages between him and Lisa Page from August 2016, which looked very much like the others at first. It was flirty in places and very angry in others. Eventually, the two got around to talking about the election, as they always seemed to do. At the time, Donald Trump had just wiped the floor with the other Republican candidates at the first debate. He was gathering steam in the middle of the country, and polls were starting to reflect his appeal with voters. Strzok had been talking about "Russian collusion" for days. He was obsessed.

In his testimony before Congress, the disgraced FBI agent turned himself into a pretzel because he couldn't explain what his texts to Page really meant. What Strzok can't explain away is this: When the FBI was ordered to turn over every communication that Strzok and Page had initiated using their government phones in January, the texts ran to hundreds of pages. These pages included even the most banal conversations—about work, people in the office, what was on television that evening—but whatever

Deep State desk jockey at the FBI put them together failed to include one thing (and only one thing): the infamous we'll-stop-it text.

Why, you might ask, out of thousands of messages, would that one be excluded? If you believe the guy who put it all together, it's the result of a technical error with the printer. Apparently, some glitch in the circuits kept the most incriminating piece of evidence from being revealed to the public, and it took another sweep of the phones by the inspector general to reveal it. While the IG was investigating, however, Peter Strzok was becoming one of the most powerful men in the government, issuing subpoenas and deciding how the investigation against Donald Trump should proceed. In other words, he was in a pretty good position to try to "stop it."

Lisa Page left the Mueller team early, and Peter Strzok was removed from it in August, almost exactly a year after he had vowed to stop Trump on his government-issued device. Of all places, he was transferred to the human resources department, which we always thought was a dumb place to send someone caught sleeping with a subordinate. But the damage Page and Strzok did—along with the three other people who were found to have strong anti-Trump leanings—is enough to render the investigation invalid. Anything Mueller's investigation may turn up will be tainted.

Of course, the IG report wasn't the first we'd heard of the sexting. They'd been public since January. What the report did, however, was firm up the timing a bit and let us see exactly how those texts matched up with their actions. Just after Strzok sent his "congratulations" message about the first woman being nominated to a major party, for example, he began dragging his feet with the Clinton email investigation so that the woman would never be convicted of a crime.

He also spread rumors around the FBI building that there was absolutely nothing to Hillary's emails, and that everyone should be more worried about the Russians coming in and trying to steal the election.

Months later, when Strzok testified in front of Congress, he would imply—yell, actually—that it's impossible for one person's bias to influence the actions taken by the entire Federal Bureau of Investigation. He'd tell Congress that there are too many safeguards, too many other people working in the building, to let one person get in the way of conducting a fair investigation. If this were 1985, we might agree with him. Back then, the FBI really did operate independently of the executive branch, and there was no bias toward establishment figures over outsiders. As we've written elsewhere in this book, the FBI was designed long before the administrative state had put a chokehold on the American political system. The bureau has been as susceptible to corruption and politicization as any of the other agencies. What's the use in having "so many other people" in the building, after all, if all those people believe exactly the same thing?

The investigators from the inspector general's office also turned up three more employees—although they're not named in the report—who sent messages to one another in support of Hillary Clinton and against Donald Trump. Two of these agents were dating, and they later married one another. The other was a staunch supporter of Hillary, who sent messages with her government-issued cell phone and email. And these are just the people who used their government devices to send the messages. We can only imagine how many special agents at the FBI held similar views but were smart enough not to discuss them on their work phones.

The IG undoubtedly was thinking along the same lines. In the executive summary of the report, he recommended that the FBI add a "warning banner" to all the government phones it issues. The banner would remind the agent that they should have "no reasonable expectation of privacy" when using the device.

There were plenty of other issues the IG report uncovered. For instance, James Comey and Peter Strzok both used private email servers to conduct government business, thereby hiding their conduct from the public just like Hillary Clinton. It seemed they were abiding by their own fake policy, which makes that an acceptable thing to do. There was the Midyear Exam team's failure to ask Clinton any questions of consequence when they interviewed her.

The report was damning enough, we thought, to warrant a full-scale housecleaning at the FBI and other agencies. It proved once and for all that the intelligence community has become a hyperpartisan arm of the liberal Deep State, and that no one inside should be trusted implicitly with conducting a fair investigation. Still though, we hoped the report would signal the beginning of the end of the Russian investigation. We weren't close to being right.

Although it was far from what we'd expected, the IG report released on June 14, 2018, exploded in the press. Reporters and staffers on the Hill were flipping through it in the morning, looking for the juiciest bits and trying to speculate on what was going to happen. We both got so many calls from reporters that our phones nearly blew up. As the day wore on, however, it became clear that nothing would change. By noon, every liberal media outlet in the country had found a way to get ahead of the narrative, saying the report actually exonerated Comey and the FBI. Much like Comey had done for Hillary Clinton a year earlier, they said that although his conduct had been "careless" and perhaps "reckless" it wasn't illegal. After all, they seemed to say, hadn't Comey suffered enough at the hands of Donald Trump? Shouldn't we wait for his memoir to come out in paperback before we start judging him? It only took one day before we realized how entrenched the Deep State had become.

That realization was right in front of us. It was in the pieces of the report that the IG hadn't meant to investigate. Horowitz didn't see, or didn't want to see, any problem with the fact that thirteen of the lawyers on Mueller's sixteen-person team are registered Democrats, or that the other three are left-leaning "independents." He didn't see any reason to look into the fact that Bob Mueller, who was rejected for a job by Donald Trump the day before he started investigating him, might have a conflict of interest. It is true that the inspector general's orders were to investigate only the FBI's handling of the Clinton email case, but given how intertwined that case is to the phony Russia investigation—and how urgent the timing is—calling Horowitz's decision not to broaden the scope of his investigation curious is the understatement of the century.

We knew that nothing the IG report found would have been enough, and that the proof we needed was in the hands of Congress. All the president had to do was release it to the public.

CHAPTER 17

PLEAS AND VERDICTS

ON THE MORNING of Tuesday, August 21, 2018, Corey got a phone call from the president. They spoke for a while about a couple of things, including Paul Manafort, whose verdict would likely be in by lunchtime. Corey knew Paul Manafort was a rat from the second he strode up to the dinner table at Mar a Lago in his yachting outfit, but he didn't say so to the boss. President Trump was still sympathetic to Manafort, and believed he was being treated unfairly by the FBI. The jury, however, was of a different opinion.

Paul's jury had been out for three days, but rumor was that they had reached a verdict on at least a few of the eighteen counts leveled against him. President Trump echoed what he had tweeted, that Paul had been treated very unfairly.

"I'll see you on the plane this afternoon?" the president asked.

Corey paused. President Trump and a small team—Dave included—would be taking a trip that afternoon to Charleston, West Virginia, where the boss would be speaking at a rally for Patrick Morrissey, the West Virginia attorney general whom he'd endorsed in the U.S. Senate race. Corey, however, wouldn't be with them. The president had told Corey he wanted him to take the trip with them a couple of times, but Corey was in New Hampshire and couldn't make it. Besides, the runway in West Virginia was pretty small, so the team was taking a scaled-down version of Air Force One to accommodate it. The plane would be packed—it was just a matter of deciding who to pack it with.

"What?" he said. "Who told you you couldn't come? I want you on that plane this afternoon."

"Dave will be making the trip with you, sir." That made the boss happy.

When the president hung up, Corey went back to his Twitter feed for the news. The speculation about a verdict in the Manafort trial was wall-to-wall.

As he looked at his feed, Corey took a brief moment to appreciate the irony of the situation—that he, the man who'd been summarily fired by the Trump campaign for being too inexperienced and deferential to the candidate, was being asked to come aboard Air Force One for a private conference with the president, while the man who'd replaced him was being tried for eighteen different federal crimes in a Virginia courthouse. There is no irony quite like political irony, he thought.

Dave drove to the White House to join the motorcade to Joint Base Andrews for departure on Air Force One.

* * *

At Joint Base Andrews, raindrops began to bounce off the tarmac. Light thunder rumbled overhead. Marine One was grounded, and the president was taking the Beast to the runway. This set takeoff back a few minutes.

As Dave stood on the tarmac waiting to board, the voices around him were reaching a consensus, reporting that the Manafort verdict was in and would be announced at any moment. There was speculation as to how many of the crimes he'd be convicted of and how heavy the sentence would be. But no one doubted it would be bad for Manafort, and by extension the White House.

In his head, Dave ran over the eighteen crimes Manafort had been charged with before the trial—which, among other things, included bank fraud, perjury, and tax evasion.

If they write the true history of the fake Russia investigation, one of the main public relations problems for the Trump campaign will stand as Paul Manafort.

Dave boarded the plane and took a seat at the conference table. On the far wall, the flat-screen television was tuned to Fox News, and they were running file footage of Manafort. That photo, at least, was enough to make Dave wince. But the verdict was coming, and what made things worse was that Michael Cohen, Donald Trump's longtime personal lawyer, was in federal court in Manhattan, where the media was reporting he had struck a plea deal. Dave looked around the cabin. Johnny DeStefano and Hogan Gidley were both traveling on Air Force One. Stephen Miller was working at the table on the president's speech for that evening.

A few minutes before takeoff, the mood in the cabin was somber. Everyone seemed to be working or chatting with one eye while keeping the other fixed on the television.

The steward announced that the president was about fifteen minutes away. Dave and Brad Parscale, President Trump's 2020 campaign manager, kept their eyes on the screens, talking about that night's rally and the Senate race to pass the time.

Then, at exactly 4:52, the first bit of news came. With a backdrop of a Manhattan courthouse, a Fox News anchor informed the passengers on Air Force One that Michael Cohen, dressed in a blue suit, described as "President Trump's personal lawyer," had just pled guilty to eight separate criminal violations. They went on to say that he was forgoing his right to trial as part of his plea deal. He had told the court, according to the broadcast, that he had committed each of the eight violations. Clearly, the New York prosecutors cut a deal for less jail time for Cohen in return for him implicating President Trump in his crimes. The prosecutors who received the referral from Bob Mueller wanted to make sure that Trump—the man who had attacked the investigation on Twitter, fired James Comey, and began to expose the special counsel for the partisan witch hunt that it was—would be implicated somehow.

The speaker crackled again. The president was five minutes away.

Before anyone could begin speculating about the implications of Cohen's plea, there was another breaking news bulletin. This one was spoken over camera shots of a different courthouse in Alexandria, Virginia, where the jury in Paul Manafort's trial had just returned with a verdict. The newscaster announced that Manafort had been found guilty on eight counts of fraud and conspiracy, and that the judge would declare a mistrial on the other ten counts. As if that weren't bad enough for Manafort, he was facing a second trial in a few weeks on additional charges. Manafort ended up cutting a deal with the prosecutors on the additional charges and skipped the second trial altogether. He pled guilty to additional charges and will serve a maximum of ten years in jail for his crimes.

Within minutes, Manafort was back in a tiny cell and the liberal hosts of the major networks were practically jumping for joy. The networks, which had been keeping the Russia hoax story running on fumes for almost two years, now had enough fuel to run it until the midterm elections at least, or until the power went out in their studios.

Hogan Gidley and Brad Parscale, who were President Trump's constant link to the world of the media, started preparing for the president's arrival. When the voice came over the loudspeaker and announced that the president had arrived, no one knew what to expect. Everyone assumed he had gotten the news, but no one was sure how much or when.

President Trump came in as usual, walking slowly, greeting Cory Gardner, the U.S. senator from Colorado, who began to tell him about the particulars of the U.S. Senate race in West Virginia. The president always wanted to know the granular details of any event he was a part of, and the rally for Morrissey was no different. Looking at him, Dave wondered whether he had gotten the news at all. It was almost as if nothing had happened. But before anyone could ask what he was thinking, the president turned to Parscale, who was sitting on a couch across from Dave. He spoke calmly, as if he was asking about the bad weather or a dinner menu.

"How's this all playing, Brad?"

Everyone knew what he meant. The television was still playing in the background, but Trump didn't look at it. President Trump, as always, wanted to know what people were saying, and how it looked from the outside. Dave appreciated in that moment that in addition to being the constant subject of the Fake News coverage, Trump was an avid consumer of the news. He was as interested in the shape of the narrative as anyone else. For Donald Trump, it's always about the story. The reaction of his audience is important to him. He cares about his audience and he always sees the big picture.

Brad told him about some of the initial reactions he'd seen on cable—that most weren't great, but it wasn't looking apocalyptic or anything. President Trump portrayed no trace of emotion. He just turned and walked into his cabin. For a moment, he watched the flat-screen television from the doorway. Then he closed the door. Within two minutes or so, the plane was in the air. The news was still playing.

On Fox, they weren't talking about the end of the Trump presidency, but there was little in the news of the day that was positive, and reporting reflected that.

The ride to West Virginia took about forty minutes in total, during which time the president spoke to Senators Shelley Moore Capito and Gardner about the Senate race in their state. They advised him on the best way to beat Senator Joe Manchin (D-WV).

In what seemed like an instant, we were outside the site of the rally in West Virginia, where just about every Trump-loving Republican in the state had gathered to greet the group. Patrick Morrissey, whose campaign the president had come to support, led the pack, taking President Trump by the shoulder and leading him to the Charleston Civic Center arena, where he'd be speaking. The boss was quiet, but still smiling.

As the group moved into the holding room backstage, the governor of West Virginia, Jim Justice, had come to greet the president. The size of a grizzly bear with a jowly face, the governor has a sweet personality and southern charm that contrasts starkly with his appearance.

While visiting with the governor, the president learned that Jim Justice's thirty-seven-year-old son had suffered a blood clot and was hospitalized in Boston. The governor had flown in just for the rally, and he would be flying back to Boston as soon as it was over. Dave was close enough to hear the conversation.

"Governor, listen," said the president, lowering his voice. "Get out of here and get back to Boston to be with your son. And let me tell you: anything you need for your boy, you call me. Everything I have is at your disposal."

In that moment, Dave was back in Trump Tower in 2010, hearing the exact same words come from Donald Trump's mouth. Dave's son Griffin had had four brain surgeries and two heart surgeries around the time Dave became Trump's de facto political advisor, and it had turned his entire world upside down. At the time, he and his wife had taken to sleeping in the waiting rooms of hospitals. They had begun drawing up their schedules around doctors' appointments and making plans to go to secondary consultations. During one of their meetings, Trump asked how Griffin was doing: "Anything you need," he said. "Everything I have is at your disposal. Anything, Dave. You call me anytime."

During his son's illness, Dave had been told roughly the same thing by a dozen other people. He could tell that a few of them really meant it, while others were saying only what they believed they had to say to be nice. Even if things got bad, he never thought he would really take any of them up on it. But he never doubted that Donald Trump would make any call that he had to, reach out to everyone he knew, and use dollars from his bank account if he thought it would help Griffin get better. Dave has never forgotten the sincerity that President Trump showed him and his family.

Luckily, Griffin recovered fully, and Donald Trump helped Dave raise money for the children's hospital in Washington, D.C. Listening to him talk to Governor Justice in West Virginia reminded Dave of his own experience, and he knew that President Trump was deadly serious about helping the governor's son if needed. That's just who he is.

But the reporters and Trump supporters outside on the arena floor weren't interested in the promise to help, or the acts of kindness that seem to follow Donald Trump wherever he goes. The Fake News only wanted to intimate that Manafort's or Cohen's guilty verdicts or pleas would lead directly to the president. The supporters in the arena were only there to help Donald Trump Make America Great Again!

Halfway through the boss's speech, Dave felt like he was back on the campaign trail.

"Loyal citizens like you helped build this country," said the president. "Together we're taking back our country, returning power to where it belongs, to the American people. From Morgantown to Madison to Charleston, this great state was settled by tough pioneer men and strong pioneer women who tamed the wilderness to build a better

life for themselves and for their incredible American families...We're the smart ones, remember. I say it all the time.
You hear the elite. They're not elite, we're elite."

The crowd loved it, and Dave realized that the Manafort
and Cohen verdicts didn't matter at all—not as long as
these people were still out here. These were people who'd
watched the same news we did but didn't care what they'd
seen. They knew that the charges were bogus and the plea
deal was a coordinated attack. They didn't need convincing; they only needed someone to keep fighting for them.
Watching them, Dave found it amazing how easy it is to
believe in change when you don't spend all your time in
Washington, D.C., worrying about the next attack and preparing for assault from all sides.

Out here, in the rest of the country, there were still people who needed help—people who still worked for a living,
who'd gotten their jobs back because of President Trump's
policies and didn't want to lose them again. When it came
to the reelection, they were all that mattered. The FBI could
arrest everyone who'd ever shaken the president's hand
and force them into confessing to some fabricated crime
and it wouldn't change the fact that the American people
still need President Trump in office. They still believe in
the message he's been espousing for decades.

Ultimately, this was the message he ended on, say-
ing, "We will make America strong again. We will make
America safe again and we will Make America Great Again.
Thank you, West Virginia. Thank you."

As he was coming down the ramp at the end of the rally,
Trump spotted a man waving a red MAKE AMERICA GREAT
AGAIN hat. The president was surrounded by Secret Service

officers, who formed a kind of human shield around him wherever he went. Just getting his arm out for a handshake was a project, and technically went against protocol. But he always made a point to stop anyway, talking to as many of the voters as he could, hearing their messages of support and answering their questions.

Before the president could say anything, the hat was in midair. In one smooth motion, like he was back at first base at the New York Military Academy, where he went to school, President Trump snatched the hat out of the air. As he did, the crowd erupted in a cheer. From the very beginning, the MAGA hat had been a symbol of all he'd been fighting for. The president's eyes twinkled with mischief as he tilted his head toward the red-hat guy and yelled.

"I don't have a pen!" he said. "Do you have a pen?"

There was a Sharpie flying through the air before he could finish the sentence, wobbling for a few inches before it came to rest right in the president's palm. He signed the hat and threw it back, then shook a few more hands on his way out. The crowd was going crazy.

Nothing can stop this man and his message. Not Paul Manafort. Not Michael Cohen. Not Robert Mueller. Not even the Deep State.

Outside the venue, with the storm clouds gone and the moon shining brightly on the packed parking lot, the president turned to Dave.

"You come with me," he said.

Together, they moved toward the back door of the Beast, the armor-plated limousine that carries the president wherever he goes. Just as they were about to get inside, the president asked for Patrick Morrissey to come over. Things had been so hectic at the end, that the president hadn't gotten a chance to say good-bye to Morrissey. Dave could tell he was still wired from being onstage in front of so many people.

"You were great," Trump said. "That was terrific. Now, don't worry about coming with us in the motorcade. You stay here and campaign. I need you in the Senate."

Standing beside the open door of the Beast, the president and Dave spoke to Morrissey for a few more seconds, talking about the rally and the turnout. Even out in the parking lot, there was a kind of electricity in the air. It was something that Dave felt at every Trump rally when the sound of the rally crowds was still echoing in his ears, and the Deep State and the fake Russia probe were only a storm system in the distance. After a few seconds, the Secret Service agent gave the sign that it was time to go. Morrissey and President Trump shook hands, and Dave said good-bye and good luck. Before stepping into the limousine, the president paused and turned around.

"Patrick," he said. "This is an amazing night for you. Make sure you make the most of it."

The ride back to the airport was short, filled mostly with talk of the rally. Back on the plane, we gathered with the rest of the team and the president asked, "How's it playing?" Brad Parscale made a few remarks; so did Stephen Miller, who'd gotten a few pats on the back for writing a great speech. The president's confidence had spread to all of us and no one seemed terribly worried, even though we were heading back into the depths of the swamp. Sean Hannity was on the television in the background, talking sense and giving a good account of the day's events; Trump took a few phone calls. As we were landing, he turned to Dave.

"What do you think?" he said.

Dave, knowing how Washington, D.C., operates, gave his honest opinion.

"Well," Dave told him, "the sun's going to come out tomorrow. By then, they'll be on to something else. No matter what happens, you'll still be president in the morning."

CHAPTER 18

AGAINST ALL ODDS

AT THE END OF AUGUST, we traveled with the president to a rally in Evansville, Indiana, to support Mike Braun, the Republican candidate for U.S. Senate, against the Democrat incumbent, Joe Donnelly. We were happy to be asked and itching to do what we do best—campaign.

When we arrived at the White House late that morning, a staffer met us at the portico door to the lower level of the West Wing. By orders of the chief of staff, John Kelly, we were not allowed to be in the West Wing unescorted. In light of all we have done and what we have learned—senior advisors and staff to the president removing important documents from his desk to fit their own agenda, senior staffers recording conversations in the Situation Room, and an anonymous "senior official" in the administration writing an op-ed for the *New York Times*—the security measures applied to us were ludicrous.

As we were walking in, several black SUVs pulled up on West Executive Boulevard. Out of one stepped Attorney General Jeff Sessions. Sessions' early recusal from the Russian hoax investigation has been a constant irritant to the president. Sessions was the first U.S. senator to endorse candidate Trump. We spent many hours with Jeff on the campaign trail and during the transition. To a person, we all like him. During the transition, when the president was considering Sessions, Corey gave him a call to ask if he would accept the position if the president offered it to him. The president thought Senator Sessions would do a good job, and so he offered him the position to reward his efforts during the campaign.

Then came the immediate recusal from the Russia investigation, which took all of us by surprise but was deeply offensive to the president, because if he would have known that Attorney General Sessions was going to recuse himself he might not have nominated him for the position. Running into the attorney general that morning brought the uncomfortable memory of the recusal and the whole specter of Mueller's Russia probe to mind—not the best way to start the day.

The next thing that happened was another reminder of the permanent battle the president finds himself in—a battle with the Washington, D.C., establishment. On the way to Joint Base Andrews, the motorcade we were in pulled up to a light where a hearse and several limousines were waiting. Corey tapped Dave on the shoulder and motioned with his head for him to look out the window. Dave leaned over and looked.

"Wait . . . is that . . . ?"

John McCain had died just a few days earlier, and his funeral services, which stretched over a week, were being covered wall-to-wall in the press.

Beside us on the road was the hearse and motorcade headed to Andrews to meet the Boeing C-32A that had flown his body in from Arizona. The flag-draped casket would be placed in the hearse and driven to the National Cathedral in D.C. for the funeral.

We knew that this funeral would be the ultimate insider's event. Gathering at National Cathedral later that week would be the largest collection of former presidents, senators, Beltway lawyers, and lobbyists in recent memory.

Though the day might have been off to a rocky start, all worry seemed to fall away when we boarded Air Force One that afternoon. Something about soaring through the air with Donald Trump makes everything seem possible. With us was Stephen Miller, Johnny DeStefano, Bill Stepien, Dan Scavino, and Derek Lyons, the White House staff secretary who'd taken over for the alleged abuser Rob Porter.

The president walked in and looked around at us and the half-dozen staffers who'd come along with him.

"Dave," he said jokingly, "glad they could find a seat for you." White House staff had told Dave there might not be enough room for him on Air Force One that day. This has been a running joke between the boss and us for the past year.

Also joining us on Air Force One was Mark Lotter, the former press secretary for the vice president. He is a strong advocate on television for the America First agenda. We went wheels up around four o'clock in the evening.

The steward, Matt Miller, came over and asked what we would like to eat. The president held up a hand and asked him for a minute. "You know what, fellas?" he said. "They have the best cheeseburgers in the world on this plane. You fellas want a cheeseburger?"

Most ordered salads, including Dave, who ordered a chicken Caesar salad. Corey knew better and threw his hands up with a smile. He said, "Sir, I'm having what you're having." (Here's a tip, by the way, for any of you who might someday share a meal with President Donald J. Trump: if the president asks you if you want a burger, say you'd be delighted.)

The steward took the order from the president, which was "salad for this guy—and cheeseburgers for me and Corey."

Just like that, we were back on track. The steward headed to the galley as Air Force One rocketed us toward Evansville.

Across the street from the venue, the president sat with thirty or forty business leaders for a roundtable discussion. After the photographs with the fire and police chiefs, which the president always does, Dave and Johnny asked the president if he would take the opportunity to call North Carolina, where Congressman Mark Meadows was hosting a fund-raiser in Asheville that evening. Mark, a good friend of Dave and the president, had invited Dave to attend the event. Mark was planning on placing the president's call on speaker and holding it up to a microphone so the entire audience could hear what the president had to say.

"Absolutely," he said. "Have them set it up."

The military liaison ensures that a secure phone system is available for the president at all times. It was designed so that the president could make a call from almost anywhere in the world to almost anywhere else in the world securely. Dave provided the congressman's number to the military aide.

When Meadows answered, the staffer told him he was the military aide to the president of the United States and handed the phone to the boss. Meadows put the phone on speaker and held it in front of a microphone. We listened while the president delivered a rousing message to the crowd in North Carolina. Trump praised Mark Meadows for his hard work and support in Congress as well as his steadfast defense regarding the fake Russia investigation, and the crowd went wild. Again, Donald Trump was able to be in two places at once, phoning in his support just the way he'd done on the cable news networks during the campaign. It was a move that probably gained Meadows a whole lot of goodwill with his most enthusiastic supporters.

In the hold room, we watched a television that had the live feed showing service members carrying the flag-draped casket of Senator John McCain off the government plane and placing it into the hearse we had passed on the way to Andrews. We stood silently with the president as he watched the solemn procession play out. Out of respect, the president decided to start his rally about fifteen minutes late.

When the president then took the stage in Evansville, the audience of more than eleven thousand people went wild. The room was electric and the boss was at his absolute best, as good as any event on the campaign, but now armed with campaign promises he'd already kept.

With the audience hanging on his every word, he talked about the passage of the historic tax bill that had proven to be an enormous triumph. Huge companies like Walmart, Target, and Kroger turned tax savings into a hiring spree, adding thousands of jobs. By the spring after the bill passed, the U.S. Department of Labor announced that the job market was the best—the best—in the history of keeping that statistic. The number of Americans with jobs grew at an unprecedented rate and the unemployment number was the lowest it had been in generations.

He told them about the record number of circuit court judges he had nominated and about fulfilling his promise of moving the U.S. embassy in Israel to Jerusalem. He talked about the stock market, which had soared to record highs, with the index rising an incredible 17 percent. He told them about the federal regulations that he had cut or rolled back, and about the money that each cut put in their pockets. He told of how illegal border crossings were down 40 percent.

The applause grew louder with each accomplishment the president clicked off. This wasn't, however, a stump speech. Donald Trump doesn't know how to give a stump speech. Instead, it was pure Trump gold. He went "off glass," the term used when the speaker pays no attention to the teleprompter. He had the crowd laughing, cheering, and chanting the same chants that had reverberated in stadiums and arenas around the country during the campaign. What had been the longest of long shots back in June 2015 had paid off in the most remarkable way. The campaign had become a movement, and the movement had become historic.

Seeing the president on the stage and seeing again that look in his eyes that those of us who worked on his campaign know so well, seeing the jubilant crowd watching their champion, reminded us that President Trump is a fighter. And not just any fighter but a street fighter, a man who does whatever it takes to win. He outworks, outhustles, and outsmarts his opponents.

Donald Trump was a candidate like no other we've seen. The main reason isn't his money or his sense of humor—both of which are great. It's not even his bold, off-the-cuff manner of speaking. No, what makes him unique as a politician, and as a president, is how he reacts when people attack him. He is the greatest counterpuncher in history, taking the fight to his enemies and hitting them back three times as hard as they hit him. It is what helped him to slaughter the most accomplished Republican primary field in the history of American politics. It's what enables him to keep fending off attacks from Democrats, the media, and the establishment today.

During the debates, Trump's attack-first style is what allowed him to shine on the crowded stages. He called out blatant lies, talked over his opponents when they started being dishonest, and gave out nicknames that will stick to them for the rest of their careers. It was Trump's willingness to stand up against Washington insiders that drove people to the polls in November, and it's also what keeps people supporting him today. As long as he stays on the attack against all that is unfair and unjust in our nation's capital, his support will never waver.

But when the FBI's attacks about the phony Russia probe came, the president's first legal team advised him to cooperate completely. For a while, this was the official position of the White House. But once the full scope of Mueller's and Comey's deceptions became clear, different decisions were made. Donald Trump decided to be who he is and to do what he does best, calling out the tactics of the Mueller probe at every opportunity.

And this time, he wouldn't be doing it alone.

When President Trump first sought to hire legal talent outside his circle of personal attorneys to help with the phony Russia probe, he turned to New York attorney Marc Kasowitz before selecting John Dowd and Ty Cobb. Dowd and Cobb are both experienced Washington insiders and good lawyers, but the advice Dowd and Cobb gave to the president was to cooperate with Mueller fully. They told him if he did, the investigation would be over by Christmas 2017. As the president had nothing to hide, he was willing to follow the advice of his counsel. But when Christmas came and went, and the Mueller investigation showed no signs of stopping, the president became frustrated. By spring, he knew he had to make a move.

Things changed immediately when Rudy Giuliani joined President Trump's legal team in April 2018. The president had added a real fighter to his team. Most Americans remember Rudy as America's Mayor. He was serving his second term as the mayor of New York City on September 11, 2001, when Islamic terrorists flew planes into the World Trade Center, murdering nearly three thousand people. Mayor Giuliani's steady, steely-eyed leadership during and after the attack kept America's most populated city calm and strong. Heroic, confident, and beloved by all, Rudy was knighted by Queen Elizabeth II the following year.

What people might not know, however, was that Rudy had been a legendary anti-corruption and organized crime prosecutor as the U.S. attorney in the Southern District of New York before he was mayor. For much of the 1980s, Rudy successfully prosecuted many leaders of New York's "Commission" of organized crime. He used to joke with us that the reason they set the popular television show *The Sopranos* in New Jersey was that he'd gotten rid of all the mafia in New York.

Rudy became the "face" of the president's legal team on television, tirelessly debunking the lies the left was disseminating through the media about the phony Russia probe. During the campaign, the mayor was a regular on the networks and cable shows and he was the sole surrogate on the Sunday shows during Billy Bush weekend.

When Rudy Giuliani joined the president's legal team, he worked next to Jay Sekulow, a well-known conservative lawyer and for the past twenty-five years the chief counsel to the American Center for Law and Justice. Sekulow had been with the president from the beginning. Pat Cipollone, an experienced Washington litigator whom we had gotten to know through our mutual friend Laura Ingraham, had also joined the team. Pat joined us in New York for debate prep sessions with then-candidate Trump and brought a deep background and experience to the table.

The point person inside the White House is the famed lawyer Emmet Flood. When Alan Dershowitz heard that the president hired Flood he said that the administration was "preparing for battle." A former Justice Scalia law clerk and advisor to President Bill Clinton during his 1990s impeachment, Flood is certainly battle tested and known as a fighter who never gives an inch in negotiations. Unlike his predecessors on the Trump team, Flood wasn't about to let Mueller set the rules.

The president didn't stop there. He hired the Coral Gables, Florida–based husband-and-wife legal team of Martin and Jane Raskin. Both have experience with the DOJ. Martin led the criminal division of the U.S. attorney's office and Jane was a prosecutor for the U.S. attorney's office in Boston, where her supervisor was one Robert S. Mueller III.

The change in legal teams and strategy could not have come soon enough. Led by Flood inside the building and Rudy outside, the president was ready for battle.

We had been waiting for this moment for a long time. In May 2017, we both received calls from Michael Bowe, Marc Kasowitz's law partner. Kasowitz has been one of Trump's personal attorneys for decades. Bowe asked us to come to the White House for a meeting on strategy. Reince was the chief of staff and the meeting was held in his office. Present was Reince, Bannon, Bowe, Kasowitz, and one other lawyer from their firm. They asked us to come in one at a time. This seemed a little odd, but Corey went in first, while Dave waited in the foyer talking to the staff. Inside the room, they asked Corey how he would set up a team to deal with the Mueller investigation, what steps he would take, and if he was interested in coming inside. When Corey finally came out twenty-five minutes later, he smiled at Dave.

"It's a job interview," he said sarcastically. "You're going to want to bomb it."

When Dave went in, the same people were present, most seated at the long, twelve-seat conference table in the chief's office. Bannon, who's a stander, stood in the doorway to the Rose Garden.

In May 2017 we had begun discussions with the president and the senior staff about putting together a war room, similar to the one President Clinton had when Ken Starr was investigating him. The war room team would operate both internally and externally. Clinton mastered this approach with legal talent such as Lanny Davis, who currently represents Michael Cohen in this matter, and talented political operatives such as Chris Lehane and Mark Fabiani.

Dave sat at the conference table and just as Kasowitz began to ask a question, Dave stopped him.

"You want to talk about this, that's fine," Dave said. "But if we do, Bannon and Reince have to go."

Based on Dave's experience as a Clinton investigator, he knew that if they were going to talk about outside counsel, he didn't want West Wing insiders to hear about it.

In the end, the war room never materialized the way it should have, and in hindsight that put the team at a significant disadvantage.

The change in strategy, however, the one we had envisioned all those months ago, was now, eleven months later, being implemented. With a first-rate legal team lead by Flood, and Giuliani pounding the propaganda of the witch hunt on television, and us working as hard as we could on the outside, we believed public opinion of the investigation would turn around. Still, even with a first-rate team, it always comes down to Donald J. Trump.

The person who changed the tide of public opinion was the person with the largest microphone in the world.

Donald Trump knows that the fate of the administration and his America First agenda would not be decided in courtrooms or in pitched legal battles. It wouldn't be decided by a politically motivated investigation predicated on a phony dossier. It wouldn't be decided by the vile, Fake News. It would be decided by the people of the United States, the same people who crammed into venues in Charleston, Wilkes Barre, or Tampa, or scores of other places across the country. Those are the people who know what is true and what matters.

Those are the people who elected him president of the United States, and they won't let anyone take that decision away from them. They will continue to join Donald Trump and head straight into battle for the heart and soul of our country.

ACCOMPLISHMENTS

ON SEPTEMBER 17, 2018, business leaders and workers from around the country gathered in the Roosevelt Room of the White House for the first-ever meeting of the President's National Council for the American Worker. This was the first group of its kind, specially designed to help students, wage workers, and laborers in the United States learn new skills and achieve higher paying positions. Corporate executives from Walmart, Home Depot, and General Motors were just some of the people in attendance that day.

Before the event, the president had arranged for a lunch with some of these executives in a private dining room in the West Wing. Vice President Mike Pence also attended. President Trump knew better than anyone that when it came to making deals and crafting new policies—especially when it came to the working men and women of the

United States—it was best to sit down face-to-face with the big executives. Although not all, some big business executives are out-of-touch with their working-class employees. The lunch was supposed to be a chance for President Trump to change that—to make sure his initiatives were being implemented properly, and that things were going to move forward as expected. Even with the Fortune 500 guys, President Trump is hard as nails when it comes to the American worker, and as hands-on as it gets.

By any measure, the meeting was a success. This was one of the main reasons why Donald Trump was elected, to align business and government in the most advantageous way for the American worker. The meeting also had some laughs. The president never leads a dull meeting. This one was like-minded people united in a good idea, and all there were in a good mood.

During the meeting, President Trump had made a few propositions, among them that every small business in the United States should be retraining one or two of its employees for a higher-skilled position.

"If you do that for 30 million small businesses around the country," he said, "that starts to add up."

By the end of the meeting, a large slice of the country's largest employers were well on their way to instituting retraining for the work force and enabling the American working class, men and women, some who voted for Trump, some (a very few) who hadn't, to get better, higher-paying jobs.

As the meeting concluded, the executives and the vice president accompanied the president into the dining room. As they did, they walked past the seventy-inch television that President Trump keeps on in the West Wing. This day, the television happened to be tuned to one of the Fake News networks, which was uncommon because the president is not a big fan of Fake News. Onscreen, a reporter was talking about the chaos in the White House, saying the president was currently upstairs in the residence throwing a fit about the confirmation hearings of Judge Brett Kavanaugh or some other fake story of the day. President Trump was furious, the reporter said gravely, and that he had been screaming at aides all day. As the news camera panned out to a wide shot of the White House residence, President Trump turned to Vice President Pence, smiled and shook his head.

"Hey Mike, am I upstairs?" the president asked. "Am I furious?"

The divide between the reality of what was going on in the White House and the fabrication that was being reported to the American people was nothing new. The lies about Mr. Trump in the media began on the first day he announced his candidacy, and have increased incrementally since. On this day, though, however, the starkness of that juxtaposition of truth and fakery were side by side and on display in front of some of our county's biggest business leaders.

Everyone laughed, and they went in to have lunch.

President Trump has connected with the working classes of America in a way that no candidate since Ronald Reagan had been able to do. He fills stadiums with excited voters from all walks of life who line up for miles just to hear him speak. It was only when Mr. Trump shot to the top of the polls that the media finally caught on and began airing his rallies in full. Even then, the elitist coverage by the press treated the Trump movement like a joke, a collection of backwater rubes who would buy anything a celebrity would try to sell them. That superior, better-than-you attitude only changed on election night, when they had to announce to their bewildered liberal viewers that Donald Trump had indeed been elected the forty-fifth president of the United States. Since then, that bewilderment has turned to a toxic hatred of the president and everyone who voted for him.

If this book has shown anything, we hope it's that, as reported, news and coverage of Donald Trump and his presidency is usually wildly inaccurate. While they're telling you he's screaming at aides or throwing a fit, he's actually meeting with business executives trying to make the workplace more advantageous for the American worker. While they're telling you he's unhinged, unbalanced, or unfit, he's cogently working eighteen-hour days to make America safer, more successful, and more respected. While they're telling you he's "colluding with Russia" and "cozying up to Putin," he's bolstering the cyber-defenses of the United States to protect against election interference (something he also did on September 17, 2018, by the way). In this book, we've done the best we could to give the real story behind the Trump presidency and the enemies who try to undermine it every day, some of whom are involved in the Witch Hunt of the Mueller fake investigation, and some of whom are in the White House itself. Some of whom you see all the time on television, and some who hide behind an "Anonymous" byline.

Just like the campaign, however, we're outnumbered and outgunned. The sheer amount of lies hurled at him, the force, position, and power of those aligned against him, the sinister nature and will of his enemies is overwhelming.

And yet, against all odds, Donald Trump and his presidency not only survives but thrives.

As you have now read, President Trump has confronted unprecedented challenges during his first two years in office. The Clinton cabal created a fake narrative for their election loss, blaming it on Russian interference; the Department of Justice spied on members of his campaign and then lied to cover it up; obstructionists in Congress did everything in their power to thwart his America First agenda; and members of his own staff worked from inside the White House to stop him from succeeding. And yet through all that and so much more, Donald J. Trump continues to fight and achieve remarkable results. He has been able to accomplish more during his first two years in office than most presidents get done in eight.

Under his leadership, the stock market has soared to heights that have previously only existed in theory, and he's made it possible for more Americans to have jobs and collect paychecks than ever before. He has brought a culture of deregulation back to the United States and passed the most consequential tax cuts in our nation's history. The unemployment rate is at a record low and our trade agreements are being renegotiated to benefit the United States rather than the free riders who have been ripping us off for years. We know the Fake News will never tell you the accomplishments of this administration because it doesn't fit their narrative that the United States is in perilous times. However, we will share those accomplishments with you, and look back on some of the circumstances surrounding them.

To stop Trump from winning the election over Hillary Clinton, the FBI and DOJ—which were run by Trump-hating FBI agents—ran an operation from New York City to London to Moscow, hoping to catch members of the Trump campaign in some kind of "collusion" with the Russians. The Fake News was "reporting" that he was a racist and an unhinged maniac, digging up false stories from the past and paying their pundits to trash him on television. They pulled out the most provocative quotes from his speeches and edited the audio selectively to achieve their desired effect. Still, he managed to pull off one of the most thrilling victories in the history of American politics, by reaching voters who had been summarily ignored and sidelined for decades. And that was just the beginning.

From his first day as president, the knives were out. We now know that Deputy Attorney General Rod Rosenstein was recommending people wear "wires" while meeting with the president and discussing the possibility of invoking the Twenty-Fifth Amendment in order to remove the president from office. In other areas of the administration, members of the Deep State leaked President Trump's transcripts of his calls with foreign leaders to the press, and the press began printing them in full, never stopping to worry about the implications of their actions or taking any responsibility. The Fake News portrays a White House that is chaotic and dysfunctional, even as President Trump signed executive orders on everything from the disastrous Paris Climate Accords to deregulations to the safety and security of our nation's borders. This is when the stock market began its climb to record-breaking heights, and Trump began renegotiating bad trade deals that now bring prosperity and wealth back to American shores. He did it all while fighting a disinformation campaign so immense and widespread that even the most knowledgeable followers of the news couldn't tell what was true and what was fake.

In Congress, the fight was even harder. It wasn't only that every Democrat in the House and the Senate was dead set on voting against President Trump's America First agenda; they also managed to convince several Never-Trump Republicans to join them. Some like Jeff Flake did it for power and attention, while others did it out of fear and a desire to hold on to their seats. But the effect was the same. After a setback in the battle over Obamacare repeal—which is still going on, despite what you might have heard in the media—the president managed to pass a historic tax cut package, ensuring that middle-class families have more take-home pay and higher wages so they can attain their part of the American dream. He also confirmed more federal court judges than any president since George Washington (who had zero to begin with) and saved many small estates and family farms from the crippling death tax. Even with a healthy majority in Congress and the full support of his own party, these would be remarkable achievements. Without either of those things, they're almost miracles.

But as we've said before, you'd never know it. When all you're reading about in the news is Robert Mueller and his illegitimate Russia probe, it's almost hard to believe that Donald Trump is running one of the most effective, efficient administrations in modern history. Despite having to deal with the fake Russia investigation, Trump has nominated two Supreme Court justices, expanded services at federal veterans' hospitals across the country, and begun making good on his promise to build the wall. When

Mueller and his team were making a show of indicting twelve Russians for attempting to hack the election, the president was strengthening our nations' cyber defenses and ensuring that nothing like it could ever happen again. The media, as you might have guessed by now, reported one of those things, and totally ignored the other.

The list of what President Trump was up against during his first two years in office is long—so long, in fact, that this book, which is called *Trump's Enemies*, only scratches the surface. The same, however, goes for what he was able to accomplish during those first two years, despite a multitude of challenges that a president has never faced before. Below, we've included a copy of a list that the president sometimes reads from when he speaks at rallies and other events. Even for him, the accomplishments of his White House are too numerous to rattle off extemporaneously. This list is by no means comprehensive, of course, and it's sure to have grown by the time this book gets into your hands:

Over four million jobs created since the election, with 201,000 jobs created last month

More Americans are now employed than ever recorded before in our history

Jobless claims fell to their lowest level in nearly five decades

We have created nearly 400,000 manufacturing jobs since his election

Blue-collar jobs recently grew at the fastest rate in more than *four decades*

We've added 100,000 jobs supporting the production and transport of oil and natural gas

Economic growth last quarter hit 4.2 percent

Americans' pensions have grown more than $1 trillion in value since the election

African American unemployment recently achieved the lowest rate ever recorded

Asian American unemployment recently achieved the lowest rate ever recorded

Hispanic American unemployment recently achieved the lowest rate ever recorded

Women's unemployment has recently hit the lowest rate in nearly half a century

Lowest unemployment ever recorded for Americans without a high school diploma

Veterans' unemployment has recently hit the lowest rate in nearly half a century

Almost 3.9 million Americans have been taken off food stamps since the election

Median income for Hispanic Americans rose by 3.7 percent and surpassed $50,000 for the first time in history

The official poverty rates for African Americans and Hispanic Americans have reached their lowest level in history. The Pledge to America's Workers has resulted in employers committing to train more than 4.2 million Americans

95 percent of U.S. manufacturers are optimistic about the future—highest ever

Signed the biggest package of tax cuts and reforms in history. After tax cuts, over $300 billion poured back into the United States in the first quarter alone

Saved family farms and small business from the estate tax, or death tax

Under our tax cut, small businesses can now deduct 20 percent of their business income

Helped win U.S. bid for the 2028 Summer Olympics in Los Angeles

Helped win U.S.-Mexico-Canada united bid for 2026 World Cup

Opened ANWR and approved Keystone SL and Dakota Access pipelines

Record number of regulations eliminated

Enacted regulatory relief for community banks and credit unions

Obamacare individual mandate penalty *gone*

Trump's administration is providing more affordable health care options for Americans through association health plans and short-term limited duration plans

In the first year of the administration, the FDA approved more affordable generic drugs than ever before. And thanks to our efforts, many drug companies are freezing or reversing planned price increases

We reformed the Medicare program to stop hospitals from overcharging seniors on their drugs—saving seniors hundreds of millions of dollars this year alone

Signed right-to-try legislation

Secured $6 billion in *new* funding to fight the opioid epidemic

Reduced high-dose opioid prescriptions by 16 percent during Trump's first year in office

Signed historic VA Voice legislation and the VA Accountability Act

Expanded VA telehealth services, walk-in clinics, same-day urgent primary, and mental health care, and launched the promised twenty-four-hour veteran hotline

Increased our coal exports by 60 percent in 2017

U.S. oil production has achieved its highest level in American history and we have recently surpassed Saudi Arabia and Russia as the world's number one oil producer

United States is a net neutral gas exporter for the first time since 1957

Withdrew the United States from the job-killing Paris Climate Accords

Canceled the illegal, anti-coal, so-called Clear Power Plan

Secured record $700 billion in military funding; $716 billion next year

NATO allies spent more than $42 billion more on defense since 2016

Kim Jong Un has reemphasized his commitment to denuclearization, and the remains of our fallen warriors were returned home from North Korea

Process has begun to make the Space Force the sixth branch of the armed forces

Confirmed more circuit court judges than any other new administration

Confirmed Supreme Court justice Neil Gorsuch; Confirmed Supreme Court Justice Brett Kavanaugh

Withdrew from the horrible, one-sided Iran deal

Recognized Jerusalem as the capital of Israel, and moved the U.S. embassy

Protected Americans from terrorists with the travel ban, upheld by the Supreme Court

Issued executive order to keep open Guantanamo Bay

Concluded a historic U.S.-Mexico trade deal to replace

NAFTA. Negotiations with Canada are under way

Reached a breakthrough agreement with the European Union to increase U.S. exports

Imposed tariffs on foreign steel and aluminum to protect our national security

Imposed tariffs on China in response to their forced technology transfers, intellectual property theft, and chronically abusive trade practices

Improved vetting for refugees and switched focus to overseas resettlement

We have begun *building the wall*

Republicans want *strong borders* and *no crime*. Democrats want *open borders,* which equals *massive crime*

From looking at this list, it's clear that we could have written an entirely different book called *Trump's Accomplishments*. Considering how Fake News covers this presidency, we'd be doing the American people a service by writing it. The working men and women of the United States, however, already know that Donald Trump has been a roaring success as a president. They see evidence of that in their paychecks, their places of work, and around their dinner tables. They know that Trump is fighting the establishment every day for them. They know he's not going to stop until the administrative state and the swamp have been completely dismantled and/or drained and the rogue agents of the intelligence community have been brought to justice for their crimes against the American people.

But make no mistake. Trump's enemies, the ones we've exposed in this book and more, aren't about to stop, either. They will continue spreading their lies and subverting and obstructing the president's agenda at every turn.

We have no doubt that the next few months will be among the most consequential of the entire Trump presidency. The road to reelection has begun, and so has the fight for America's soul.

And we will be with President Trump every step of the way, helping to bring his message of strength and prosperity to the American people once again.

When it comes to President Trump, there isn't a poll devised that can predict what the future holds. We can tell you one thing with certainty, however. There is no one who will work harder to achieve more for the American people than President Donald J. Trump.

ACKNOWLEDGMENTS

We are thankful for all the professional staff of the Trump administration who are dedicated to Make America Great Again, as well as President Trump's America First Agenda.

Thank you to everyone who made this book possible, both the on-the-record sources and the many off-the-record sources who spoke to us.

To our editor, Kate Hartson, and our publisher, Rolf Zettersten, and the entire team at Center Street/Hachette Book Group. We could not have written this book without the help of our collaborators, Brian McDonald and Sean McGowan. And to our agent, Mel Berger at William Morris Endeavor: Thank you for your support of this important project.

ABOUT THE AUTHORS

COREY R. LEWANDOWSKI currently serves as president and CEO of Lewandowski Strategic Advisors LLC. He previously served as the chief political advisor and campaign manager to Donald J. Trump for President. Prior to that, he was an executive for Americans for Prosperity. Lewandowski appears regularly on television and serves as an on-the-record spokesman to major print outlets. He is a contributor to *The Hill* newspaper and serves as senior advisor to the Great America Committee, Vice President Mike Pence's PAC. Corey has spoken at Harvard University, Stanford, Oxford, and the University of Chicago. Corey previously served as a certified police officer with the state of New Hampshire, where he lives with his wife, Alison, and their four children.

DAVID N. BOSSIE has served as president of Citizens United since 2001 and is a Fox News contributor. Beginning in August 2016, Bossie served as deputy campaign manager for Donald J. Trump for President and then as deputy executive director of the Presidential Transition Team. In 2015, Bossie was ranked number two in *Politico*'s top fifty most influential people in American politics. In 2016, he was elected from Maryland to the Republican National Committee. David proudly served as a volunteer firefighter for more than fifteen years in Maryland, where he lives with his wife, Susan, and their four children.